CHARLES RENNIE MACKINTOSH
Architect and Artist

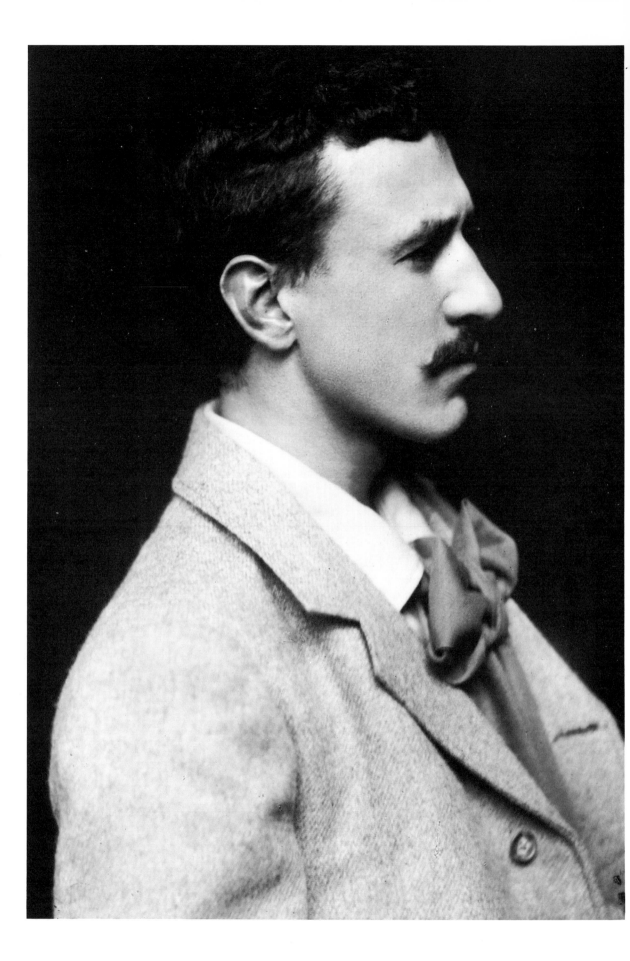

CHARLES RENNIE MACKINTOSH

Architect and Artist

Robert Macleod

E.P. DUTTON, INC.

First published, 1983, in the United States by E. P. Dutton, Inc.

Library of Congress Catalog Card Number: 82-74516

Produced by Bettina Tayleur Ltd
1 Newburgh Street, London W1V 1LH
Text set by Rowland Phototypesetting Ltd, Bury St Edmunds
Printed and bound in Great Britain by Collins Glasgow
Designed by Tom Carter
Jacket/cover design by Penny Mills

ISBN: 0-525-93296-8 (cloth)
ISBN: 0-525-48056-0 (DP)

10 9 8 7 6 5 4 3 2 1

First Edition

CONTENTS

FOR MARILYN

INTRODUCTION

There is hope in honest error; none in the icy perfection of the mere stylist. The Mackintosh aphorism, borrowed in fact from J. D. Sedding, is a key to the understanding of the great architect, but it is also a comfort to anyone setting about the increasingly daunting task of writing about him. For the past fifteen years have seen a growth of interest in the man and his works, certainly on the scale of interest shown in Le Corbusier and Frank Lloyd Wright but based, of course, on a comparatively tiny volume of work.

One of the most curious aspects of this surge of interest is that it has occurred so relatively recently, as compared with the sustained interest in the other so-called pioneers of the Modern Movement, whose work has been examined, discussed, and published at length over many decades. Indeed, it was in just this context, as a harbinger of the Modern Movement, that Mackintosh was first presented to the new generation, by Nikolaus Pevsner and subsequently by Thomas Howarth, in the only major treatments until recent years.

But the fact is increasingly apparent that Mackintosh and his works sit very uneasily in any campaign which numbered among its goals the rejection of tradition, the glorification of new technology, the rejection of ornament, and the substitution of cool generalization for intense individuality. If he intended to be modern, it was never in that way.

Perhaps this very fact goes some way to explain the new and deeper interest in him. Now that pioneer-hunting has become a recreation of the past it is possible to accept with equanimity, and with growing delight, those aspects of his work which never quite accorded with received architectural doctrine of thirty years ago. Perversely, this newer liberal appreciation brings with it the new hazard that always accompanies eclecticism, that the deep seriousness which fed his labours will be ignored in the plethora of sheer visual delights.

For Mackintosh was an intensely serious architect, deeply committed to the idea of an architectural and artistic expression for his own time, uncompromising in his pursuit of it, and utterly scornful of the glib facility which characterized so many of his contemporaries. To be distracted by the novelty and the visual loveliness of his works – and it is so easy – and to enquire no further, is to serve him less than fairly. It is perhaps no fairer than to assess his importance, as was done a generation ago, by the extent to which he used large areas of glass and unadorned white walls.

In the fifteen years that have elapsed since I first undertook to write about Mackintosh, much has occurred which is of direct relevance to this study. There are three areas which are deserving of comment.

The first of these concerns the increasingly widespread disenchantment with the Modern Movement in architecture, both among those concerned with architecture directly and among the wider public. This is not the place for a discussion of the rights and wrongs of such a phenomenon, but the fact is worth noting. For, as intimated above, there is now perversely as much interest in those aspects of his work which were *not* anticipatory of the mid-twentieth century as there used to be in those which were. Those who pin their hopes on a new vernacular revival can find much in his domestic building, his notebooks, and his writings over which to enthuse. Those who delighted in the Art Nouveau have in the meantime rediscovered Art Deco and found to their amazement that he was there as well.

The second development is one which has been gathering momentum for a number of years, and which is undoubtedly interrelated with the first: that is the increasing volume of research and publication on Victorian and Edwardian architecture and architects. The background and even the specific context to which this book refers is much more widely understood and appreciated than could have been assumed fifteen years ago.

The most important development of relevance to this study is the impressive amount of serious scholastic work which has been dedicated to Mackintosh himself. The two men most directly responsible for stimulating and encouraging much of that research are now sadly deceased: Andrew McLaren Young, late Professor of Fine Art at the University of Glasgow, and Sir Harry Barnes, for so many years Director of the Glasgow School of Art, and faithful and enthusiastic custodian of the Mackintosh legacy of and in that building. From their individual efforts and the enthusiasm of a relatively small circle in Glasgow itself another generation of admirers has added significantly to the knowledge and assessment of Mackintosh and his works.

These studies and the reflection of fifteen years have forced me to a reassessment of some aspects of my original study. The central thesis remains the same: that for an understanding of such a man and his creative activities it is necessary to understand something of the context within which he worked and what he had to say about his own work; and that for a real assessment his work must be seen for what it was rather than for what it prophesied. It may have borrowed from Art Nouveau, it may have foretold certain aspects of the Modern Movement, it may have anticipated Art Deco, but its importance lies in what it was and is, a body of paintings, furniture and buildings which continue to move and thrill us.

Apart from detailed corrections, there are two principal aspects of my study which have required re-evaluation. For the first, I am indebted to Roger Billcliffe, whose assiduous scholarship and fine judgement have done what was long overdue for Mackintosh studies. He has not only redressed the described balance between Mackintosh's architecture and his other works (where for example he has shown the sheer volume of his furnishing and interior design work, including fabric designs), but he has directly challenged the treasured Mackintosh myth. The end-of-life obscurity and near poverty are fact. But part of the romance has been that after his zenith in Glasgow, Mackintosh took to painting simply to fill his time; that the best his painting can offer us is some speculative clue to as to how his

Right Willow Tea Rooms. Doors to the Room de Luxe, 1903. The largest and richest set of leaded glass designs by Mackintosh, purposefully feminine in effect. Even here there is a hint of the rigour and spareness which were increasingly characteristic of his architectural work.

Overleaf
Left Winter Stock, Walberswick, 1914. Pencil and watercolour, 264 x 217mm
Right Hazel Bud, Chiddingstone, 1910. Pencil and watercolour, 258 x 202mm.

8

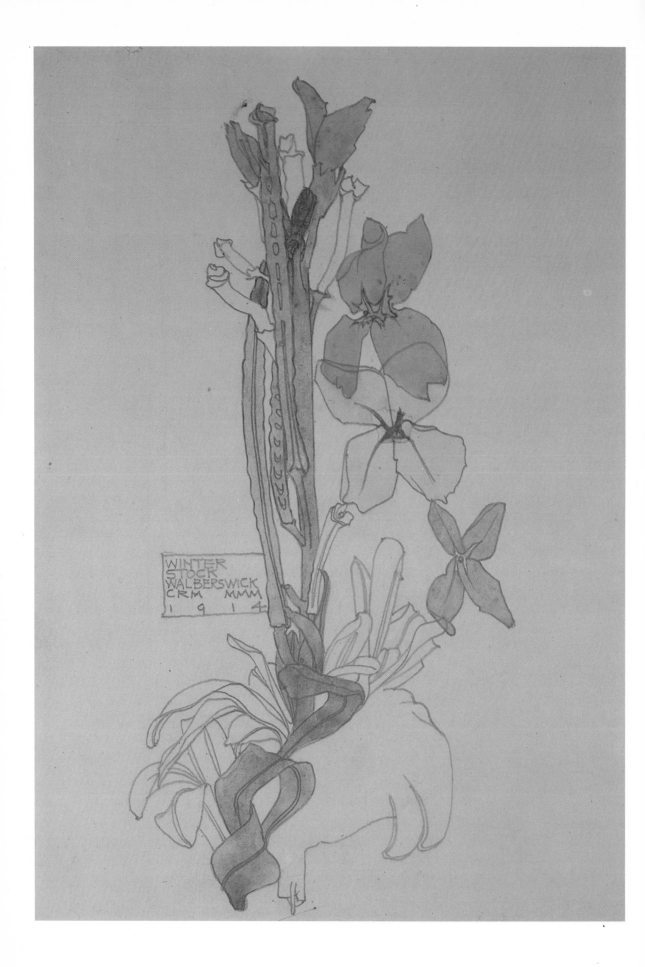

WINTER
STOCK
WALBERSWICK
CRM MMM
1 9 1 4

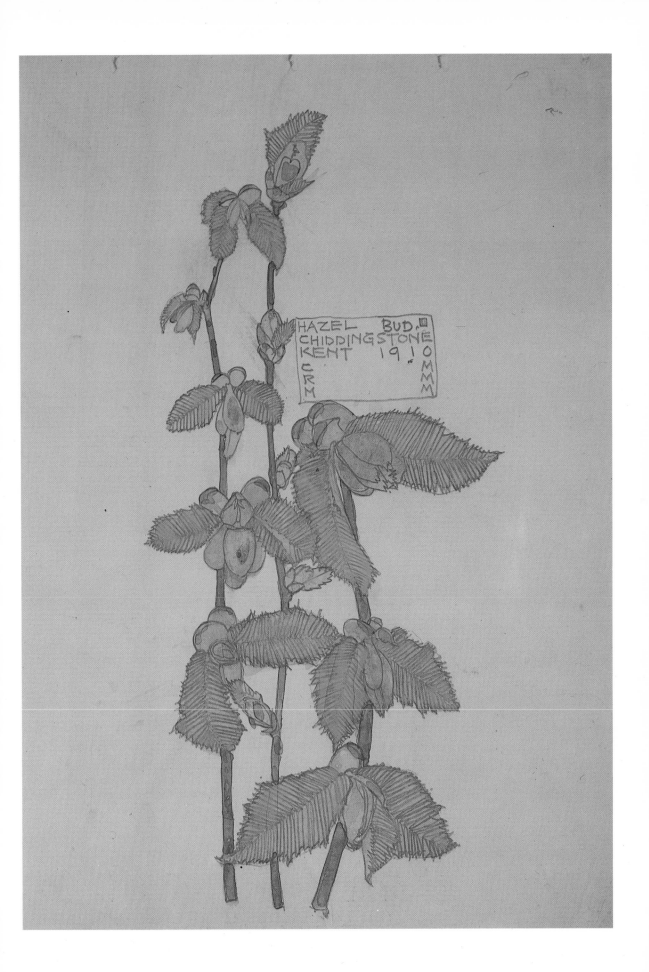

HAZEL BUD.
CHIDDINGSTONE
KENT 1910
CRM OMM

Left No. 78 Derngate, Northampton, 1916. A bedroom as reconstituted in the Hunterian Art Gallery, University of Glasgow. There are minor inevitable dimensional differences between this space and the original room.

architecture might have developed had he been given the opportunity. Billcliffe has shown us both that Mackintosh was immensely serious about his work in this phase of his life, and that we must in turn recognize its importance in its own right. These later works, in particular the paintings, are of major significance and continue in a different medium the explorations of a lifetime.

In fact, the more one examines the total body of work that Mackintosh produced, the more one is driven to the inescapable conclusion that all of the work, be it fabrics for a particular space, chairs for a particular individual, paintings, or major buildings, received the same scrutiny because they were intrinsically equally important. It is still tragic that he was unable to produce more buildings, but his productive life was neither as truncated nor as frustrating as might be suggested by an examination of the architecture alone.

A further reconsideration of my original study is the result of the work of several people on the Mackintosh architectural works and drawings. David Walker has published several detailed accounts of the buildings, particularly in Scotland, of Mackintosh's antecedents and contemporaries, which not only provide a much fuller picture of the scene in which he worked, but suggest a variety of specific sources for some of his formal treatment, particularly in the earlier years. The publications and lectures of the Charles Rennie Mackintosh Society since 1973 have provided much new material on Mackintosh and his contemporaries.

In my attempt to set Mackintosh in a real context in his own time, it has been suggested that I failed to describe adequately the variegated vitality of the Glasgow architectural scene at the turn of the century. This is probably true, although the differentiation between fine threads of influence, and in particular those who influenced him as apart from those whom he influenced, can become a task of diminishing profitability. The self-evident thesis that he was extraordinary in whatever context remains unchallenged. Having said that, it remains important to reiterate the fact that all genius, including all architectural genius, always comes out of a real context. The greatness lies more in transformation than in creation, and this is as true of Frank Lloyd Wright, Le Corbusier, or indeed Michaelangelo, as it is of Mackintosh. If, therefore, I have served Mackintosh badly by not fully delineating the local context, redress must be made. The most effective redress that can be made without distorting the entire structure of a modest narrative is to draw the attention of those interested in a fuller picture to the appropriate publications of recent years. Where relevant to my theme, I have referred to new material in the present text. The sources are as listed in the select bibliography.

There is an issue of architectural historiography which is becoming of increasing concern, and it has tended to become more, rather than less, acute in recent years. My original study assumed a view on this, albeit implicitly, but it is now perhaps time to raise it more overtly. It concerns the matter of stylistic attribution. The discovery of specific forms in the work of one architect, repeated in the work of another who must have been exposed to the work of the first, is an exciting and tempting event for the researcher. But the causal attribution that one is tempted to make must be tempered with caution. The late Professor W. G. Howell once made the remark in private correspondence that the designer of the Fylingdales radar domes had undoubtedly seen a golf ball during the course of his life, but the fact was not necessarily of direct relevance. Similar forms can recur for different reasons. At any particular time, certain favoured forms are 'in the air', sometimes as the generalized solutions for topical problems, sometimes for specific iconographic reasons, and sometimes for felt, more than thought, impulses. Without such, indeed, we could not usefully talk of the Styles of Architecture. During a period of great diversity, such as the one under consideration, family similarities between artists are of great importance, for they tend to tell us something of the sympathies of their authors. But without specific evidence such as the declared loyalties of the artists themselves, or the specific iconographic intent, direct attributions may be positively misleading. For architectural design was then and remains now emphatically not the abstract composition of forms on paper or in space, but the increasingly complex resolution and reconciliation of a wide range of conflicting demands, in an increasingly attenuated process.

Of course, where some wholly new or particular formal attribution can be made, our understanding may well be advanced. The identification and subsequent analysis of the shield forms on the railings of the Glasgow School of Art by Hiroaki Kimura, for example, is a dramatic case in point. We are given here conclusive evidence of a Mackintosh preoccupation which goes far beyond the superficial influence which had tended to be assumed in the past.

Other surprises of this kind may await us in the future with respect to Mackintosh. Further minor building works may yet emerge. But the danger that looms is that unnecessary effort will be expended in scouring the works of his contemporaries for formal attributions which cannot be confirmed, and which cannot advance our understanding of the man or of the qualities of his architecture. This is in no way to detract from the valuable work which has been undertaken by such people as Dr Frank Arneil Walker and others on the fascinating Scottish architecture of the period; it is to say that this work is of value in its own right and not simply as a seed-bed for grafts on to the Mackintosh tree.

To state that the architecture of Charles Rennie Mackintosh is of international consequence is to state the obvious. The growth of the Society in his name, the constant round of pilgrimages made to Glasgow from all points of the globe, and the continued literary efforts undertaken on his work are compelling evidence. But one of the heartening aspects of this interest is perhaps not so obvious.

He first came to public attention as one of a varied, by hindsight remarkably varied, constellation of 'pioneers' of modern architecture. But two things have occurred to alter that image for the better. The first I have already noted – the questioning of many aspects of 'modern' architecture as it has been progressively revealed during recent decades. The second is much more important. For as more and more people have had the opportunity to see his work at first hand, the more they have come to appreciate the power and vision of his buildings in themselves.

Here one must note a number of changes that have occurred during the last few years that have made the range of his work so much more accessible to the public at large. The Glasgow School of

Art, which has been mercifully under sympathetic care for all of its life, continues so. The present Director, Professor Anthony Jones, and his staff, like their distinguished predecessors, continue to make it available to the endless round of people who come to look and admire, while carrying on with the task of maintaining a fine working school in a remarkable tradition. The Charles Rennie Mackintosh Society, established in 1973, has now a permanent home in Queen's Cross Church, and not only provides all that can be imagined of his graphic work in reproduction, but also sponsors an excellent and scholarly Newsletter, provides information on access to his buildings, sponsors tours and events, and maintains the building in a highly sensitive way. What could so easily from its inception have been an inward-looking, nostalgic organization of a rather 'precious' kind, has developed through wise counsel and enlightened leadership into a model for any urban community. 'Toshie' would have been very proud.

During recent years, the Hill House in Helensburgh passed from the late private owner, Campbell Lawson, into the hands of the Royal Incorporation of Architects in Scotland, and more recently to the National Trust for Scotland. It was typical of the sensitivity and foresight of the last private owner of that great house that it should have been passed on to good and caring hands. Its future now seems assured, and it is available to a wider audience.

The Willow Tea Rooms in Sauchiehall Street have been sensitively restored. To find in the commercial heart of a great city such a remarkable reversion, after more than half a century, of a small building that had all but disappeared, and to find it so effectively carried out, is a moving experience.

Gallery in the Willow Tea Rooms as restored by Keppie Henderson and Partners, Glasgow, in 1980. This painstaking reconstruction, described by Geoffrey Wimpenny of that firm in CRM Newsletter No. 24, is as faithful to the original as is possible today.

No. 78 Southpark Avenue, Glasgow, 1906. *Above, left* The dining room, and *Right* the drawing room, as reconstructed in 'The Mackintosh House' within the Hunterian Art Gallery, University of Glasgow.

As if this were not enough, one of the most contentious projects related to Mackintosh has now been completed. I recall conversations some fifteen years ago with the late Professor Andrew McLaren Young regarding his determination that the Mackintosh home, at 78 Southpark Avenue, should be incorporated as completely as possible in the new Hunterian Art Gallery. It was clear at the time that the original building could not be saved. William Whitfield, the architect for the new Gallery, has recreated, with as much of the original fabric as was practicable, the principal interiors of the Mackintosh home, as well as several other exhibition spaces. The outcome is, in my view, wholly successful.

It is now possible, therefore, to see at first hand a representative range of Mackintosh buildings and interiors in a way that was not possible just a few years ago. Through the happy inclusion of part of the Derngate interior and furnishings in the Hunterian, it is also possible to glimpse a vision of what the later years might have produced in architectural terms. That tantalizing glimpse describes, far better than any words, 'what might have been'.

To return to the famous Mackintosh quote with which I began this essay, it is increasingly likely that one will commit error in any description of the Mackintosh saga. For the research talent that has now assembled in Glasgow is formidable in the extreme. Against that, I have not attempted to describe all of the Mackintosh architectural works, and there may be omissions which some will question. But the intention of this study is, as it has been, to attempt to understand his work in the light of what he himself said about it, and to reaffirm his greatness in his generation.

CHAPTER ONE:
BACKGROUND

The architectural scene in Britain in 1890 was full of promise. Throughout Europe the young and the adventurous were watching British developments, emulating British achievements and imitating British fashions. And, although unknown at that time, there were easily a dozen young architects on the thresholds of their careers who were by their idealism, energy and gifts capable of bringing that promise into reality.

Yet the promise was never fulfilled. The initiative passed quickly and unmistakably to the Continent and to America. The most nearly complete survey of the work of that period remains to this day *Das Englische Haus* (Darmstadt, 1902), one of a series of critical reviews by Hermann Muthesius, who had been sent to Britain in 1896 as a cultural attaché to the German embassy. The work has only recently been made available in English translation. And of the dozen or more young heirs to the promise, only one achieved anything like international recognition. That one exception was Charles Rennie Mackintosh, and in the contradiction, enigma and frustration of his own career are crystallized the turmoil and lost opportunities of a whole generation.

To understand the life and work of Mackintosh, it is first necessary to understand something of the architectural background which he and his contemporaries inherited. It is also necessary to refrain from seeing him as a forerunner of anything until this background is established. For the tendency to identify the architectural intentions of Mackintosh and many of his British contemporaries with those of twentieth-century developments, although not entirely without cause, has obscured their stated intentions, and has left many aspects of their executed work quite inexplicable to modern eyes.

In almost every respect the development of architecture in Britain during the nineteenth century was unique and, characteristically, insular. The reasons were varied. Britain's traditional historic and natural geographic isolation was abetted by her industrial and financial superiority, and what had been, in other times, a marked sense of cultural inferiority became a startlingly aggressive nationalistic pride. In terms of architecture, it was not nearly as complacent a pride as has sometimes been suggested, and in the latter part of the century there were many voices raised in misgivings over the directions in which architectural developments were moving. But even the sternest critics did not suggest that British architects should look abroad for the solution to their problems; the main, almost the entire, emphasis was on the British condition and on British history.

A great many factors had contributed to this state, but by far the most important of these was the train of ideological development set in motion by Augustus Welby Northmore Pugin. It is now unfortunately assumed that, whenever the name of Pugin is introduced, those of John Ruskin and William Morris will follow in rapid succession, as a kind of Victorian architectural liturgy. But it is not generally appreciated how fundamentally Pugin changed the course of British architecture, entirely apart from the influences of these other very important men. Pugin's great contribution to architectural thought focused on the relationship between architecture and the society which produced it. According to him, the quality of architecture was directly dependent on the quality of the society from which it originated; and the social quality with which he was essentially concerned was *morality*. Thus his central proposition, that good architecture can only be produced by a good society, gave rise to the infusion of moral attributes to building and the continuing use of such terms as 'truthful expression' and 'honest structure'. In fact, Pugin codified, to a remarkable degree, the doctrine which has subsequently been known as 'Functionalism'.

The fact that Pugin's social message was generated by his fervent Roman Catholicism, and that his architectural message was clothed in an equally intense medievalism, did not limit his influence to the confines of the Gothic Revival. But it was because of the enthusiasm for all things Gothic in the mid-nineteenth century, and more particularly because of the enormous influence of the Ecclesiological Society, that Pugin's ideas had such widespread effect.

The Ecclesiological Society began its existence in 1839 as the Cambridge Camden Society, in sympathy with, and in some respects a product of, the Oxford Movement. It was concerned with the reform of liturgy and all the artefacts of public worship, including building, within the Church of England. Although an unofficial organization and the subject of violent attack from both the Evangelical party and the Nonconformist denominations for its sympathy with and emulation of Roman Catholic forms, it achieved through its organ, *The Ecclesiologist*, a widespread influence on the architectural profession. The ecclesiologists frankly and avowedly based their criticisms and recommendations on Pugin's principles; on, for example, his rules that 'there shall be no features about a building which are not necessary for convenience, construction, or propriety', and 'that all ornament should consist of the essential construction of the building'. They concurred with his strictures on the imposed symmetry of classical or 'pagan' architecture, and with his distaste for the equally mannered asymmetry of the Picturesque. They argued together by precept and by example that the disposition of internal spaces in the building should be demonstrated by its external forms, and that the disposition of doors and windows should be the result of considerations of access, orientation, light and ventilation – not the elements of pictorial composition.

But more fundamentally, the ecclesiologists concurred with Pugin's view of the relationship between architecture and society. And because of the religious views which they very nearly shared, they saw in both the society and the architecture of the Middle Ages – particularly that of the second half of the twelfth century and the first half of the thirteenth century – a standard which had never subsequently been matched. Accordingly, they proposed that architects

All Saints, Margaret Street, London, by William Butterfield, 1849–59. This church, virtually contemporary with the Crystal Palace, was sponsored by the Ecclesiological Society as a model urban church.

must revert to the forms and skills of 'the ancient builders' as a stylistic and technological basis; that this would take, by the most optimistic estimates, one or two generations, and that until it was accomplished there could be no basis for further exploration or unprecedented invention.

But the facts of Victorian life, in the event, proved too much for even the militant dogmatism of the ecclesiologists. By 1846 they had publicly embraced the doctrine of 'Development'. This doctrine meant simply the engrafting of other forms, of foreign details, of

modern technology, on to thirteenth-century English Gothic architecture. What it meant in terms of a new architecture can be seen in Butterfield's All Saints, Margaret Street, London, of 1849. It is English thirteenth-century Gothic architecture, built on an impossible urban site, with non-medieval accommodation – such as a Sunday school – with a German Gothic spire, using London stock bricks, and containing exposed cast-iron beams and Georgian sash windows. The result was manifestly High Victorian, scarcely 'Gothic', but – it must be stressed – anything but irresponsible eclecticism.

The influence of the Ecclesiological Society and of their two major architect members, William Butterfield and George Edmund Street, can scarcely be overestimated. For Pugin himself, in spite of his great abilities and immense energy, could never have had anything like the same pervasive influence on Victorian architecture. He was too fanatical in both his religious position and his medieval commitment, too unwilling to adapt to the needs of the society in which he found himself, and, finally, too short-lived. But the ecclesiologists were able to graft his principles on to the stock of the established Church, subsequently to dilute the archaeological fidelity of the forms in which these principles were clothed, and to adapt them to the requirements and techniques of Victorian society.

This influence was not limited to the field of ecclesiastical architecture, for the Pugin arguments were enlisted in the strenuous dialogue between the 'Gothic' and the 'Classic' camps in the so-called Battle of the Styles. The Goths maintained that theirs was the only style which could be called truly national and indigenous, that it was based on a rational exploitation of building structure and not on an abstract vocabulary of decorative forms, and that (on the principle of development) it was infinitely adaptable to the new and changing demands of the modern society. The emphasis was entirely on the national and the rational.

The Classicists found themselves compelled to reply on the same terms, and the result was inevitable. Ultimately both camps found themselves unable to justify strict fidelity to their respective styles on rational grounds and, by 1870, what direct confrontation there had been between the two had effectively disappeared. What remained was the abstracted legacy of Pugin: a compulsion to establish continuity with some native tradition of the past, and to justify that continuity on the grounds of its flexibility and rationality. It is not therefore surprising that there began in about 1870 a revival of the style of 'the brick architecture of Queen Anne and the early Georges', and that this revival was led by men, almost all of whom had begun as convinced Gothicists.

One of these apologists for the Queen Anne was J. J. Stevenson (1831–1908). He argued for the new style clearly on Puginian lines:

The style in all its forms has the merit of truthfulness; it is the outcome of our common modern wants picturesquely expressed. In its mode of working and details it is the common vernacular style in which the British workman has been apprenticed, with some new life from Gothic added.

And, to underline the social link and the indigenous basis on which this new style was founded, Stevenson recommended for Scotland the adoption of the 'Scottish Baronial' style. Essentially, all the serious architectural effort that took place for the remainder of the century was founded explicitly or implicitly on these theoretical

All Saints, Margaret Street, London. Interior of the nave and chancel.

lines. And although some architects moved towards a more rigid and academic classicism, and some to a more colloquial folk idiom, the final appeal of all was to function and native tradition.

The Pugin influence was not confined to the larger questions of style. Such architects as Butterfield and Street had demonstrated in their work a new methodology of design; an approach that was, as it were, from the inside out, where building forms genuinely were not composed according to either classic order or picturesque imbalanance. Indeed, there is often in their work a kind of gauche quality, a deliberate awkwardness that is demonstrably antipictorial. It was an approach founded on the tenets of 'truth', 'honesty' and 'reality'. And as the style pendulum swung up through the English Renaissance, it carried with it a growing expertise in free and unprecedented planning and in technological skill.

This technological skill was given great impetus by the contributions of William Morris and the Arts and Crafts movement. For their emphasis on the revival of old skills and techniques, related to the life and enjoyment of the workmen, included, of course, architecture. The Society for the Protection of Ancient Buildings had become, according to W. R. Lethaby, a 'veritable school of building', and under the guidance of Philip Webb had gathered and disseminated a formidable amount of knowledge of building technique and the behaviour of materials. With such men as Webb the inevitable happened, and the question of 'style' became almost irrelevant; if a thing were done well and rationally – responding to climate and site, and using native materials – it would assume a valid style quite naturally and unconsciously. But this was not to say that earlier stylistic idiom must be avoided; a free and wide-ranging eclecticism was positively encouraged, provided the elements were 'assimilated'. Webb, referring to this phenomenon in England's past, described it as 'insularising any imported motives. To my seeing there came a sea-change almost instantly on landing, to any fresh fashion adopted from elsewhere'.

It is readily apparent that in this context, where stylistic idiom had become an infinitely variable element, not central to architectural doctrine, in those buildings restricted by size or economy it could virtually be eliminated. And this is what had happened. From the time of the High Victorian Gothic Revival and the parsonages of Butterfield and Street, there had been a continuous tradition of simple domestic building, virtually without decorative embellishment. These buildings must be seen for what they were – from the Butterfield parsonages and the Red House by Webb to the houses of Voysey and Baillie Scott – as one end of a range whose other end often incorporated the most bewildering eclecticism.

This, then, was the architectural picture in 1890: a loose, free empiricism, at its best refreshingly direct, inventive and uncluttered; at its worst simply a chaotic pastiche of borrowings from many times and places; but always, at its best, characterized by a relaxed absorption of both past tradition and current possibility. It was a situation which could not have come into being but for the educational and professional circumstances in Victorian Britain.

The British architectural profession, unlike its European counterparts, notably that of France, had no formal system of education. The customary pattern was an apprenticeship or a period of articles of three years to a practising architect, for which the aspirant either paid his employer, or at best received little emolument. The system was as good or as bad as the capacity and sense of responsibility of individual employers. There were not a great many places in the country where this informal training could be supplemented by part-time classes. The Architectural Association established in 1862 a 'Voluntary Examination Class' in response to the Royal Institute of British Architects' inauguration of a voluntary examination for architects, but it was not until 1882, when examination became obligatory for Associateship of the Institute, that training began to be systematized. This was still, of course, on the basis of evening classes. The Royal Academy held architectural lectures, and from 1870 had a full-time architectural master, R. Phene Spiers. But it was not until the last decade of the century that architecture began to be recognized in Britain as an academic discipline. While there were undoubted drawbacks in this situation, one of its great merits was that British architecture could never have become bound by an academic sterility, or a single, central platform of patronage. It remained a fluid battleground, where debate and divergence could proliferate, and any able man, no matter how humble his beginnings, could build his platform or win his spoils.

Architectural developments in Scotland during the nineteenth century, while forming part of the total picture described here, yet retained some national differences. Classicism, in its neo-, romantic and picturesque forms, held a much stronger grip here than in England throughout the century, notably in Edinburgh. This was partly the result of a slightly self-conscious scholastic tradition – Edinburgh's claim to being the 'Athens of the North' – but also undoubtedly due to the irrelevance of post-Pugin Gothic Revival ideology. An architectural appeal founded on a return to pre-Reformation religion and society could not have the same impact in Scotland as in England. None the less, the existence of the strong Gothic Revival contingent in the south did draw from the Scottish Classicists a response in kind, as had happened with their English counterparts. This response could, on occasion, be violent – as in the instance of George Gilbert Scott's executed design for Glasgow University. Among those who objected to this Gothic invasion of the north was the great Glasgow architect, Alexander 'Greek' Thomson. In 1866 he addressed the Glasgow Architectural Society, using the occasion as the opportunity for a three-pronged attack on the Gothic Revival, the unfortunate architect, and the building design. Interestingly, one of his chief grounds of attack was on the 'constructive skill' displayed in medieval building. He acknowledged the skill as indisputable, but as being founded on 'an egregious error . . . . All the parts of Gothic architecture seem to aspire at standing upon end'. Then, widening his field and warming to his task, Thomson went on: 'But perhaps this violent conflict of forces, this incessant struggle between stick and knock-down, may account in some measure for the favour which the style has obtained with a cock-fighting, bull-baiting, pugilistic people like the Anglo-Saxons.'

Such a level of confrontation between 'Goth' and 'Classicist', while highly entertaining, could no more continue in Scotland than in England, and the result was that a common meeting-ground was found ultimately between the two, in the Scottish Baronial style, and the ideological basis of this style, like the Queen Anne in the south, was founded on premises which grew out of the Gothic Revival. The

Scottish Baronial prototypes were the latest buildings which could honestly, though perhaps mistakenly, be regarded as completely indigenous, and not foreign importations. They could therefore be used as the basis for 'development' of a true and national contemporary architecture. They also possessed, as did the Queen Anne, evidence of a kind of adaptability, of 'invention', which enabled their chief characteristics to be adapted to various modern functional requirements without violating the essence of the style.

In this self-conscious working out of a national destiny, the same wide-ranging eclecticism became apparent as had emerged from the Queen Anne revival in the south; in some cases it meant merely the addition of a few 'corbie-stepped' gables to the familiar amalgam of Italian Renaissance and 'modern' Gothic details, while in others it meant the thoughtful examination and sympathetic exploitation of national and rational building materials, forms and methods.

Perhaps the simplest and most direct of such work was that produced by James Maclaren (d.1890) and by his successors, Robert Watson and William Dunn. Such buildings as the farmhouse, steading and cottages at Glenlyon in Perthshire by Maclaren and the hotel at Fortingall (1891–2) by Dunn and Watson are fully as deserving of attention as the better known Voysey houses in the south, and stand in the same ideological succession.

This, then, was the bewildering, uncertain, yet curiously promising architectural scene into which in 1889, at the age of twenty-one, came Charles Rennie Mackintosh as a newly qualified architect.

Right, above Inn at Fortingall, Perthshire, by W. Dunn and R. Watson, and *Below* Cottages, Fortingall, Perthshire, by James Maclaren. In buildings such as these, and the simpler works of Robert Lorimer and others, the indigenous historical tradition is clearly evoked.

Below Farm-steading, Glenlyon, Fortingall, Perthshire, by James Maclaren.

CHAPTER TWO:

1863-93

Charles Rennie Mackintosh was born in Glasgow on 7 June 1868, the second son of a family of eleven children. His father was a superintendent of police, and the family life in a Glasgow suburb seems to have been normal and uneventful. Charles apparently indicated from an early age a desire to be an architect, and after the normal period of schooling, he was articled, at the age of sixteen, to the firm of John Hutchison in Glasgow.

In this same year, 1884, Mackintosh enrolled as an evening pupil in the Glasgow School of Art. Mention has been made of the relatively primitive state of architectural education in Britain at this period, and that which Mackintosh enjoyed was fairly typical. The philosophy behind it was roughly based on Ruskin's premise that architecture is the art which 'so disposes and adorns the edifices raised by man . . . that the sight of them may contribute to his mental health, power, and pleasure'. That architecture was essentially an art of adornment few questioned; and so it was that the young student spent his days learning the problems and technicalities of raising edifices, and his evenings learning the arts of adornment.

The one atypical aspect of Mackintosh's education was the institution itself, the Glasgow School of Art, and its head, Francis H. Newbery. Since the late 1870s there had been a lively interest in the visual arts in Glasgow, much of it focused on a number of young painters, who, in spite of considerable disparity in their painting, techniques and interests, became known as the 'Glasgow School'. Local collectors had been buying important French and Dutch paintings before the work of Millet, Corot or the Maris brothers had been even recognized in the south, and the influence of all these, together with the Pre-Raphaelites and Whistler, is evident in the Glasgow painters' work. This interest was inevitably reflected in the local art school, particularly after the appointment in 1885 of Fra Newbery at the age of thirty-one. Newbery, an Englishman, brought to the school considerable administrative ability, direct knowledge of developments in London, great respect for the work then current in Glasgow, and an even greater respect for creative individuality. Under his direction the Glasgow School of Art became during the 1890s perhaps the finest in Britain, and drew to itself considerable attention from the Continent.

There were three main constituents in late Victorian architectural ideology which received emphatic attention in the Glasgow school under Newbery. The first of these, owing its importance to the

Charles Rennie Mackintosh.

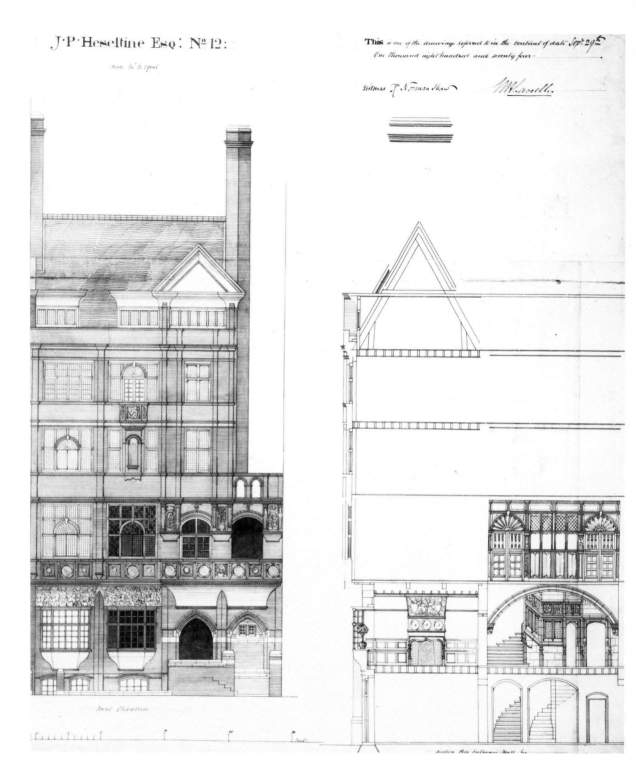

Front Elevation

obsession of John Ruskin, was the idealization of 'Nature'. Nature was to the rational the true 'reality'; to the humanist it was the substitute for the Divine; to the artist it was the inspiration for his beginning and the measure of his achievement. The designer, in whatever medium, was sent to Nature to learn principles of structure, of line and form and mass, of texture, of colour, and of fitness to function.

The second constituent was the emphasis on material and technique, which sprang directly from the Victorian emphasis on labour.

No. 196 Queen's Gate, London, by R. Norman Shaw, 1874, designed for J.P. Heseltine. Contract design drawing. Although the house as built differed slightly from this drawing, it illustrates the amalgam of features that were referred to as 'Queen Anne' at the time.

It was the doctrine of Carlyle, disseminated by Ruskin, and applied by Morris. Carlyle said:

For there is a perennial nobleness, and even sacredness in work . . . Properly thou hast no other knowledge but what thou hast got by working; the rest is yet all a hypothesis of knowledge.

This general proposition was preached by Ruskin in relation to artistic endeavour, and finally codified by Morris as the very essence of Art: 'That thing which I understand by real art is the expression by man of his pleasure in labour.' This emphasis on the nature of artistic labour led certainly and inevitably to a close preoccupation with techniques and materials, with both the old ways and the new capacities. Particularly in the applied arts, the decorative forms and motifs which were inevitably drawn from nature began to be modified and abstracted more and more in acknowledgement of the methods and media which had brought them into being.

The third constituent of the late Victorian artistic and architectural scene was the changed attitude to history and historical style. It might be termed the principle of absorption. Whereas earlier in the century historical styles had been seen as fancy dress to be assumed with consistency, but arbitrarily, or as the vehicle of an ideological allegiance – as with the Pugin phase of the Gothic Revival – they were seen in late Victorian times as one continuously relevant source-book, where elements from disparate parts of the world and epochs of time might usefully be joined. The underlying conviction was that the conscious and unconscious editing and filtration of the artist's mind would give them a modern relevance and internal consistency.

Thus in the mid-1880s these three ideological constituents were beginning to produce, through their interaction, certain common design characteristics which laid the foundation for a modern style. And it is the prevalence of these ideas which goes a long way towards explaining the otherwise puzzling fact that elements of the *style moderne*, or Art Nouveau, began to appear simultaneously among artists who had no mutual contact, and often little mutual sympathy.

A further ingredient which linked many of those who became identified under that loose and often ambiguous label of the Art Nouveau was also present in Glasgow to a significant degree. It was an enthusiasm for Japanese art.

William Buchanan has outlined in the CRM Newsletter No. 25, Spring 1980, the surprising extent to which the enthusiasm for Japanese art was widespread in Glasgow from the early 1880s onwards. The direct impact of this work on Mackintosh will be discussed in due course, but it is perhaps important here to note the fact of such widespread interest. For apart from its direct effect on the Glasgow painters, it provided a receptive context for the work of Whistler and, in due course, Beardsley. If one adds to this the current interest in Celtic art and symbolism, it is not difficult by hindsight to see the ingredients in the work of the 'spook school' which emerged after 1890, in the work of Mackintosh, his friend and fellow student Herbert MacNair, and a group of their fellows.

But there was one further ingredient which was central to the work of these young artists which must be emphasized, for it was to have critical importance in the later developments in which they became involved. It was the impulse, almost the compulsion, to devise something unmistakably *modern*. A style for the time must be found.

By and large, there is no hint in Mackintosh's student work, either in architecture or painting, between 1884 and the completion of his articles in 1889, of the precocious individualism which was so soon to set him apart. He did, however, demonstrate marked facility in both directions, and won a number of school prizes for both painting and architectural work. In 1888 and 1889 Mackintosh won national prizes for designs of a chapel and a church at the Art Training School, South Kensington, which sponsored annual national competitions for students of architecture; of these schemes only the plan and section of the latter survive, and they are not of great interest. But in the following year, after he had completed his articles and joined the firm of Honeyman and Keppie, he entered for and won the Alexander (Greek) Thomson Travelling Scholarship. Again, the design is not of much importance. The conditions were of the typical Beaux Arts variety: 'a public hall to accommodate 1000 persons (seated), with suitable committee rooms, the design in the Early Classic style, and for an isolated site'. Mackintosh's solution is a competent though entirely typical student exercise in Beaux Arts planning encased in a slightly uncertain Scottish variant on Greek revival vocabulary.

The competition award was of considerable importance to the young man, for the £60 prize financed an Italian tour, and it is from this point that it is possible to follow his ideological development in detail and with certainty.

In February 1891, immediately before his departure for Italy, Mackintosh read a paper to the Glasgow Architectural Association entitled 'Scottish Baronial Architecture'. The ideals and architectural allegiances expressed in it are not reflected in his student work; hardly surprising, for the world of student competitions was then treated with a hearty cynicism, and the nature of designs submitted generally bore more affinity with the known tastes of the jurors than with those of the authors. But in this paper are to be found in embryo all the architectural preferences and intentions which governed his mature work. The first and clearest of these is, of course, his choice of subject, a subject 'which has never as far as I remember been more than incidentally touched on within these walls, a subject indeed dear to my heart and entwined among my inmost thoughts and affections . . .' The introduction becomes yet more fulsome, and perhaps a little pretentious, but it is the pretentiousness of the maiden speech, and through the lapsed years it is still possible to sense the unease of the youth addressing his elders for the first time. None the less, it is not possible to dismiss these expressions of 'deep and filial affection' lightly; his life's work has given them in retrospect a meaning and poignancy beyond the power of his words. For the work that Mackintosh produced in his career, by which his reputation was established, was, within his terms of reference, in the Scottish Baronial tradition. To understand this, and ultimately to understand his work, it is necessary to look carefully at his view of the native tradition which he treasured so highly.

It was . . . the architecture of our own country, just as much Scotch as we are ourselves – as indigenous to our country as our wild flowers, our family names, our customs or our political constitution.

Here, in debt to Pugin and Ruskin, is the foundation of 'valid' style – its relation to the land and the society in which it grows. But Mackintosh had carefully qualified his interpretation of 'indigenous'. He pointed out that many of the features of the native style may well have originated elsewhere, but they had become native by 'absorption'. Thus he did not deny that many Scottish Baronial features were of French origin, but argued that they had been assimilated and modified to suit Scottish materials, climate and attitudes; that in many cases they had probably sprung up virtually simultaneously in France, England and Scotland to meet demands common to all the cultures. Similarly, he argued that the great Greek and Roman revivals of the nineteenth century were irrelevant; that they had been rigorously imposed from without, and that they had never been 'absorbed' into the native idiom. The argument owes its origin to Pugin, and is virtually identical with J. J. Stevenson's plea of exactly twenty years earlier, for the adoption of the Queen Anne style in England. At that time, too, Stevenson had, with remarkable prescience, argued for the adoption in Scotland of the Scottish Baronial style on the same grounds. Thus Mackintosh was not presenting a revolutionary document in any sense.

In his qualitative assessment of the Scottish Baronial achievement, Mackintosh revealed his personal architectural values in more detail.

In the castles of the 15th century . . . every feature was useful. In the 16th century also, however exaggerated some of the corbels and other features might be they are still distinguished from the later examples of the 17th century by their genuineness and utility.

This emphasis on 'genuineness and utility' is marked throughout the essay and is accompanied by a clear belief in the planning of the building being the generator of its architectural form. Thus:

. . . a very marked tendency towards symmetry is gradually creeping in . . . The door is placed as nearly as possible in the centre, and wings or towers are placed so as to balance each other. But there is evidently a difficulty experienced in reconciling the internal arrangements with the external uniformity. This period of decline although it teaches the architect no artistic lesson directly emphasises the moral that you should not take a plan wholesale and try to fit on an elevation in another style . . .

But the main lesson of the Scottish Baronial style lay for Mackintosh in its contemporary relevance:

Since then [the seventeenth century] we have had no such thing as a national style, sometimes we have been Greek, sometimes Italian and again Gothic. . . . It is a matter of regret that we don't find any class of buildings but domestic in this style, whether the style can be developed beyond this or not is a point which our forefathers left for us to decide. From some recent buildings which have been erected it is clearly evident that the style is coming to life again and I only hope that it will not be strangled in its infancy by indiscriminating and unsympathetic people who copy the ancient examples without trying to make it conform to modern requirements.

Almost certainly, it was the work of Maclaren and Dunn and Watson to which Mackintosh was referring, in suggesting that the style was 'coming to life again'. These buildings, with their studied elimination and evocation of the baronial links with touches of corbelling, or tower forms, and crow-stepped gables are the precise starting-point from which Mackintosh was to develop his own domestic designs.

In February 1891 Mackintosh left Glasgow on his 'grand tour'. He arrived in Naples on 5 April. His diary, which has survived, covers the period from his arrival in Naples, followed by visits to Palermo in Sicily, then Rome, Orvieto, Siena, Florence, Pisa, Pistoia, Bologna,

Ravenna, Venice, Padua, Vicenza, Verona, Mantua, Cremona, Brescia, Bergamo, Lake Como, and Milan to his departure for Pavia on 7 July. His return through northern Europe is not recorded, but on the evidence of the diary together with the mass of drawings produced, the pace he set himself was formidable. He rose each day between 4.30 and 7.30 in the morning, and filled the time with tramping, looking, drawing and recording. Sundays were – perhaps surprisingly – given over to attending Presbyterian or Anglican church services, if such were available, and writing letters. The cryptic observations of the diary are perhaps a more telling picture of his impressions than the more polished report he gave to the Glasgow Architectural Association on his return, and, brief as they are, provide a fascinating glimpse into a lively, witty and extremely perceptive mind.

The most striking thing about the diary is the extreme catholicity of taste displayed. There are, however, certain patterns discernible. He showed a greater interest in 'invention' than in academic brilliance; thus enthusiasm for Michelangelo, respect for Palladio; and an inclination to prefer the early work – Romanesque, Gothic, Byzantine – to developed Renaissance building. But the one building which seems to have drawn from him a really negative response was Siena Cathedral:

To begin with the front is a fraud as it gives no indication of the interior. Then when you examine the design you find that it is almost *not there*. Then you begin to see that were it not for the fine material the whole thing would be very poor as a composition. . . . So much for the front. Then the sides, well they take the cake. There are no windows in the aisles so this part is plain and might look well so, but it wasn't good enough for the Sienese. No they must have windows, so they painted windows along the wall, designed and painted in the Gothic style. Very beautiful examples, and it is a pity that the rain is wearing some parts of them away.

This is the writing of a man who had not only read Pugin and Ruskin, but who had made their architectural premises his own. The architectural concepts of 'truth' and 'reality' in building were, from the beginning, part of Mackintosh's creed.

His reaction to Siena was not entirely negative, however. He expressed general approval for the campanile and great delight in many details in the cathedral:

The floor, of inlaid marble, is really magnificent, and makes one sorry that it is a floor. It is partly covered up. . . . There are some fragments of the ancient sgraffito work in the opera which will make your hair stand on end. Figures drawn with shadow only, white or cream or ivory marble ground and shadows a pale and sympathetic green plaster or cement.

Siena received, in fact, perhaps through its initial affront to his architectural sensibilities, far more detailed attention in the diary than any other building. And the attention indicates his perceptiveness, as in his reference to the stalls:

Then the wooden stalls are really very good, one half late Gothic with just a feeling of Classic about them and the other pure Renaissance. They are undoubtedly good but like most Italian wood-work, they are very stony. Not designed like wood, but stone.

Mackintosh sent home a selection of his sketches for inclusion in the Annual Exhibition of the School of Art Students' Club, and was

S. Gustorgio, Milan, from Mackintosh's Italian sketchbook, 1891. The elegant, economic line and the searching analysis of the three-dimensional form, as well as the decorative detailing, anticipate his mature studies and sketches.

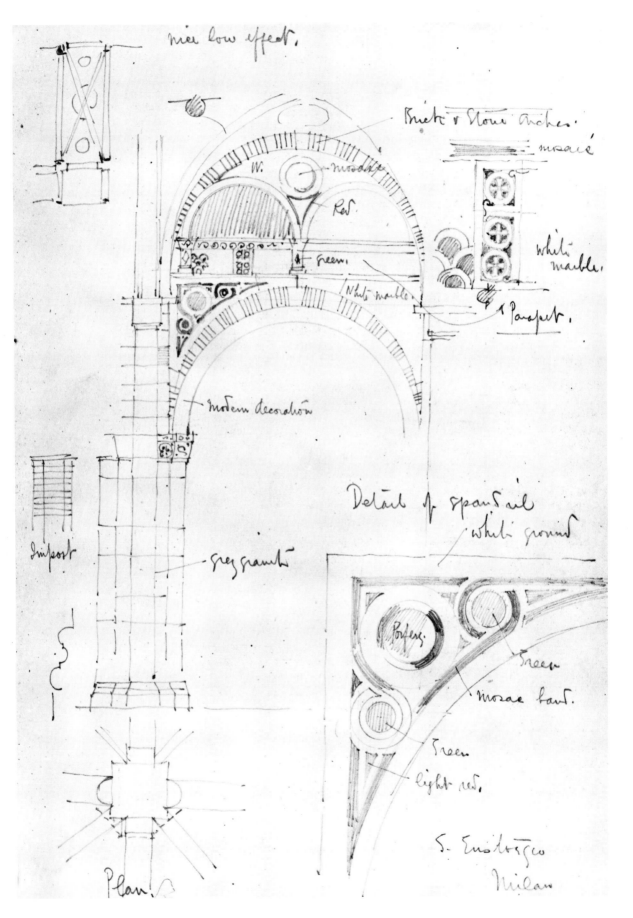

nice low effect.

Brick & Stone Arches.
mosaic

W.   mosaic

Red.

Green.

White marble.

white marble.

Parapet.

Modern decoration.

Impost.

grey granite.

Detail of spandril
white ground

Porfery.

Green
mosaic band.

Green

light red.

S. Eustorgio
Milan

Plan.

awarded first prize. And it was from this event, and these drawings, that his abilities came specifically to the attention of Fra Newbery. From this point on, Newbery's influence as friend and patron had the most important consequences in Mackintosh's life.

On his return from Italy, Mackintosh continued in his employment with Honeyman and Keppie, and with his evening studies at the School of Art. At the same time he embarked on the first of two successive submissions for the Soane Medallion competition. The subject of the 1892 competition was a chapter house. His solution was in an idiom very much in vogue at the time, a sort of free early Italian Renaissance with Byzantine flavouring, the whole articulated within a clearly defined structural frame. The most dissonant element in the scheme is the overtly 'picturesque' band of false dormers around the parapet, but their extreme linear attenuation gives a hint of the kind of graphic playfulness which was to characterize much of his mature building. Apart from this element, there is a new certainty of handling evident, and a clearly expressed structural discipline. Although unsuccessful in the Soane Medallion competition, this

S. Agostino, Bergamo, from Mackintosh's Italian sketchbook, 1891.

design did obtain for Mackintosh a National Gold Medal at South Kensington later in the year.

The subject of the 1893 Soane Medallion competition was a railway terminus, a subject which demanded a good deal more of the designer in planning and organization than the previous one had. As with his earlier student schemes, Mackintosh produced a design formally arranged around a series of major and minor axes, formal and monumental, but clothed this time in a variety of what was called 'modern Gothic'. The modern Gothic style was in itself a curious phenomenon of the times; it belonged neither to the rampant eclecticism of the broad stream of current work, nor to the purism of the earlier Gothic Revival. It tended to be used primarily, and not surprisingly, for ecclesiastical work, and two of its chief practitioners were G. F. Bodley (1827–1907) and J. D. Sedding (1837–91). It was based on rather later Gothic models than had been favoured by the Ecclesiologists – late 'perpendicular' Gothic was once more respectable – although it embraced other historical elements on the familiar principle of 'absorption'. But the chief interest of the modern Gothic of the eighties and nineties was the remarkable extent to which a genuinely unified and homogeneous style had emerged. It produced in this period not only such new devotees as Giles Gilbert Scott and Sir Ninian Comper, but, as a by-product, yet another strand for the fabric that became Art Nouveau.

A hint of this can be seen in the Mackintosh railway terminus project, particularly when compared with some of his later work. For

Below and *Overleaf* Railway Terminus scheme for the Soane Medallion competition, 1893. The influence of the 'late, flat' Gothic is very clear and the forms have many family similarities to the work of, say, Leonard Stokes. They also anticipate Mackintosh's mature style of the Liverpool Cathedral competition.

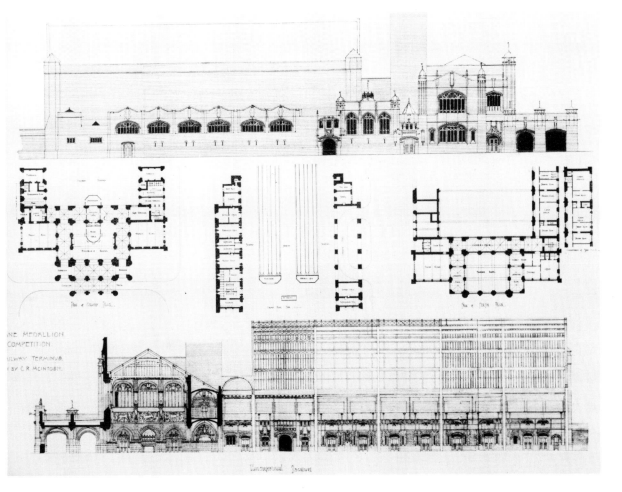

it is easy to see in the flatness and linear attenuation of the great brick surfaces, and the concentration of curvaceous detail around the windows and turret heads, how with little further convolution and abstraction from historic Gothic forms it would become an entirely typical Art Nouveau design. A design from which Mackintosh almost certainly drew inspiration was that by Henry Wilson (a pupil of, and the chief successor to, J. D. Sedding) and T. Phillips Figgis for the Ladbroke Grove Free Library which was published in *The Architect* of 20 June 1890. Not only does it embody the particular motifs that Mackintosh employed – such as the slender corner turrets – but with its strained symbolism and transitional detailing, points, albeit uncertainly, in the direction in which he was to move. A further evidence of this can be seen in a Honeyman and Keppie design of the previous year. This was one of two unsuccessful submissions for the Glasgow Art Galleries competition, and the elevational detail shown was drawn by Mackintosh, although it is doubtful if he was responsible for much beyond this scale. But in the window tracery, and particularly in the patterns of the smaller windows, virtually fully developed Art Nouveau forms are evident, within the modern Gothic framework.

These two Soane Medallion competition schemes are chiefly of

Railway Terminus scheme for the Soane Medallion competition, 1893.

The Ladbroke Grove Free Library, by Henry Wilson and T. Phillips Figgis, 1890. The large openings, ogee capped pilasters, and the symbolism of the 'Tree of Knowledge' growing up the centre pier and repeated elsewhere, indicate the influences that were catching the eye of Mackintosh and his peers during these years.

value as the only actual evidence surviving of the young architect's professional development prior to 1893. Their stylistic disparity gives little enough indication of his mature work; hints there are, and mannerisms, but the road on which he was to travel was yet far from clear. He had, however, made a small but real student reputation; he was undoubtedly a 'promising young man'. He was employed in a firm which appreciated his abilities, and in which his responsibilities were widening. He was pleasant, gregarious and articulate. He was passionately involved with his craft, and if obdurate and self-willed, his energy, idealism and marked abilities made these qualities acceptable to those around him.

House at Gartmell Fell, Windermere, by C.F.A. Voysey. This is typical of the mature Voysey manner. One of the respects in which Voysey did not influence Mackintosh was in the gross inconvenience of much of his planning. This House is characteristic.

CHAPTER THREE:

1893-96

It seems to me that to produce any satisfactory work of art we must acquire a complete knowledge of our material and be thoroughly masters of the craft to be employed in its production . . . go to Nature direct for inspiration and guidance. Then we are at once relieved from restrictions of style or period, and can live and work in the present with laws revealing always fresh possibilities.

The speaker was C. F. A. Voysey, recorded in *The Studio* magazine for September 1893.

The sentiments are readily recognizable, and although at that time his reputation rested chiefly on wallpaper and decorative designs, he had already produced more than one house in what became his typical mode. These houses, with their plain white walls, low-pitched roofs with overhanging eaves, and long horizontal groupings of windows, have often been seized on as obvious precursors of twentieth-century architecture. But the fact, as has already been noted, is that they were firmly embedded in the tradition of simple vernacular building that reached back through the parsonages of Butterfield and Street to the social ideology of Pugin. And there were others at this time in Scotland, such as Maclaren and his successors, Dunn and Watson, whose designs were equally simple and direct. By the early 1890s there was a clearly emergent fashion for such work, and Voysey, with his undeviating single-mindedness, took the lead in this mode. The relative uniqueness of Voysey's position rested on two factors: first, that his architectural output consisted almost, though not quite, entirely of relatively small-scale domestic building in non-urban settings; and second, that his art leaned emphatically on the principle of elimination, rather than 'absorption'. He was greatly, and almost obsessively, insular. This emphasis on elimination produced at its best work that was refreshingly direct and serene, and at its worst, particularly in his two-dimensional designs such as wallpaper, work that bordered on the childish.

The impact of this work, with its emphasis on craft and Nature heightened by its comparatively ruthless simplicity, was considerable. And from its inception in 1893, *The Studio* became the chief vehicle for its dissemination. At the same time *The Studio* had other eggs in its basket, all of which were enthusiastically received by Mackintosh and his fellow students. Mrs Newbery, the wife of the School Director, recalled forty years later the publication of *The Studio* as the first epoch-making event in Mackintosh's artistic development, and there can be no doubt that the work illustrated in

Endpiece to *Salomé*, Aubrey Beardsley (Elkin Mathews & John Lane, 1894). The elegance of line, the balance of dark and light and the infusion of symbolism had a major effect on The Four. What clearly did not influence them was the malevolence and sexuality of Beardsley.

that year, including Aubrey Beardsley's illustrations for Oscar Wilde's *Salomé*, and a painting by Jan Toorop entitled *The Three Brides*, had a decisive effect.

At about this time – precisely when, it is not possible to say – Newbery noticed in the work of two sisters, day-school pupils, a remarkable similarity to the work of Mackintosh and Herbert Mac-Nair. Thus Margaret and Frances Macdonald were brought to the attention of the two young men, and the four young designers came together for the first time. They were soon christened 'The Four' through the distinction and similarity of their work. Mackintosh and MacNair, who was articled at that time to Honeyman and Keppie, had been developing their graphic interests together. How far they had developed a distinctive manner by this time it is not possible to say, but it is certain that the arrival on the scene of the Macdonald sisters, together with the confirmation and incitement of *The Studio*, provided the necessary impetus for the establishment of a fully fledged style. It is clear that this style, from 1893 onwards, was indebted to the Pre-Raphaelites, to the Japanese, to the Arts and Crafts movement, to Whistler, and to Beardsley; but it was indisputably something quite different from all of these. In essence, it took the products of two schools of thought which regarded themselves as mutually exclusive, and effectively married them.

The stream of development which is represented by the Pre-Raphaelites, the Arts and Crafts movement, and, in fact although not in person, Voysey, was built around the idea of the artist's primary responsibility to society.

Indeed, that view was so central that it led in the case of William Morris and others to a programme of social reform that quite overwhelmed their artistic activities; but even those who, like Voysey, had no sympathy for the social views of the Morris group, held virtually identical views on the role of artistic activity in society. The arts must embellish, adorn, teach and elevate society by their form, their content, their manufacture and their use. The arts must stand for moral uplift, for permanence, for quality. And the inviolable mainspring of the arts was Nature.

The other stream, the so-called Aesthetic movement, embracing Whistler and perforce the 'Japanesque', as the fashion was sometimes referred to, and Beardsley, was founded on the premise that the artist owed duty only to himself and to his art, that he was above and outside the constraints of an essentially philistine society. Similarly, while nature could provide an effective source, Nature was something quite different. It could be much closer to subjective experience than to the perceived world. On this basis the only criteria for assessment were the personal aims of the artist and the qualities of his art. Thus the arts could be – in society's view – immoral, irrelevant and ephemeral.

Although these views were diametrically opposed, and the philosophical distinction is easily made, it would be foolish to suggest that all the practitioners who were influenced by these leaders made such a clear-cut distinction, and it is equally certain that these young Glasgow designers did not see their activity as bridging the two. But in no other work of the period is there such a balance between the subjective and the objective; between the simple fidelity to material and method of Voysey, and the linear contortion and convolution of Beardsley; between the moral realism of Burne-Jones and the mystic abstraction of Jan Toorop. This is not to suggest that the drawings, decorative panels, and posters produced by 'The Four' from 1893 onwards were in any sense 'great art'. Much of the work was ephemeral in the extreme, much of it was reducible to a simple

Below, left Poster for the Scottish Musical Review, 1896.
Below, right Repoussé metal plaque 'Gloria in Excelsis Deo', c1893–6. Symbolism in the service of music and religion.

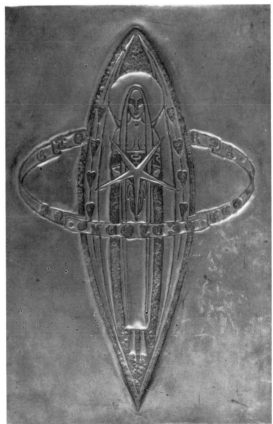

formula which was repeated with varying success – of rigid rectilinear organization, with extreme vertical emphasis, attenuated and
stylized animal-vegetable forms, and colour serving only as muted
accents. But it had an inward coherence and consistency which
entitles it to the distinction of a Style, and it provided, in the case of
Mackintosh, the basis for later and more significant development.

It is without question that Mackintosh saw his graphic activities
primarily as only one aspect of the larger question of architectural
design. He had made this point emphatically himself, in a lecture
delivered in February 1893, that is, two months before the first issue
of *The Studio*.

Architecture is the world of art and as it is everything visible and invisible
that makes the world, so it is all the arts and crafts and industries that make
architecture . . . architecture is the synthesis of the fine arts, the commune
of all the crafts.

In fact, this quotation is a direct plagiarism, as are many parts of this
lecture, of a book published in the previous year, *Architecture,
Mysticism and Myth* by W. R. Lethaby. What makes the plagiarisms
somewhat embarrassing is the fact that they have been invariably the
only written statements in Mackintosh's hand on which subsequent
historians and apologists have seized to indicate his prophetic thinking. None the less, it is important to avoid distraction from the
ideological issue, which was that Mackintosh was prepared to sub-
scribe to the ideas and to make them his own. Lethaby's book, his
first independent work, was frankly mystifying to most of his friends
and contemporaries, yet it was very important in the history of
architectural theory. It was probably the first attempt to explore
factually the ideological origins of architectural form, to move
outside the niggling contemporary preoccupation with localized
styles, to explore the metaphysical basis for the phenomenon of
'style'. It is no small indication of Mackintosh's own manner of
thinking that he, virtually alone of the architectural profession,
should have been so clearly receptive to a work of this kind.

Although he made rather too free use of Lethaby's phraseology –
all of the following quotations from the lecture originate from
Lethaby – there is no doubt that Mackintosh himself was intensely
concerned with the communicative and symbolic power of
architecture.

Of the modes of this [architectural] thought we must . . . distinguish;
some were unconscious and instructive, as the desire for symmetry,
smoothness, sublimity and the like merely aesthetic qualities, which properly enough belong to true architecture, and others were direct and didactic,
speaking by a more or less perfect realisation, or through a code of symbols
accompanied by traditions which explained them.

He went on to generalize about the origins of architectural forms in
ancient cultures, and their relation to concepts of the universe; after
discussing the role of magic and symbolism in ancient sacred building, he continued (Lethaby again):

We need not suppose, however, that temples were a sum of these symbols in
all cases, if in any; but that from this common book of architecture, each
took what he would, little or much, sometimes openly, sometimes with
more or less translation, sometimes first hand, often as a half-remembered
tradition. Old architecture lived because it had a purpose. Modern
architecture, to be real, must not be a mere envelope without contents.

Thus while, with Lethaby, he would deplore the use of sham styles, of 'make believe', he did not accept that the gulf between ancient arts and the present was impassable. For the *purpose* to which he referred was still one of symbolism and of magic – albeit a magic of light, rather than of darkness:

We must clothe modern ideas with modern dress – adorn our designs with living fancy. We shall have designs by living men for living men – something that expresses fresh realisation of sacred fact – or personal broodings – of skill – of joy in nature in grace – of form and gladness of colour.

This great plea for modernity – Lethaby's again – has often been quoted on Mackintosh's behalf. But it was one which would have had a widely receptive audience in 1893, and one, moreover, that in Mackintosh's view was already obtaining a wide response among his peers:

I am glad to think that now there are men such as Norman Shaw, John Bentley, John Belcher, Mr Bodley, Leonard Stokes, and the late John D. Sedding – names most of you will never have heard before but for all that quite as great if not greater artists than the best living painters, men who more and more are freeing themselves from correct antiquarian detail and who go straight to Nature.

Now, this list of names, even if Mackintosh did not intend it to be definitive, is of great interest. The entire list, with the exception of Belcher, is made up of men who began as Gothicists. In the case of Belcher, the building Mackintosh almost certainly had in mind was his design for the Institute of Chartered Accountants, built in 1889. This building was largely, if not entirely, designed by Beresford Pite, who was in Belcher's employ until 1891 and who had begun as a modern Goth himself. And although that building is in a form of Baroque vocabulary, its spirit and organization is very close indeed to the kind of thing that Sedding and his pupil Henry Wilson were doing with the modern Gothic.

In the work of all of these men the desire to impress with 'living fancy' – to use Mackintosh's (and Lethaby's) phrase – is evident; the desire to create new symbols out of the manipulation and reordering of old forms; to establish continuity with the past, and yet not be bound by it. They were all, to a varying extent, imbued with the legacy of Gothic Revival ideology, and Bodley, Sedding, Bentley and Stokes could be regarded as being in the direct line of succession from Pugin.

In the light of this, one can understand more clearly the motivation behind Mackintosh's railway terminus scheme. And, more important, one can understand his ideological preparedness for the revelations that the publication of *The Studio* was to bring in two months' time. For in the graphic work of Voysey, and later, in his buildings, could be seen the continuity with past tradition and the reliance on nature made 'modern' in terms of dramatic simplicity, while in Beardsley he saw the basis for decorative exploration which, though using traditional elements, could create a new symbolism.

Although the evidence of these influences became immediately apparent in his graphic work, it is not quite so easy to discover their immediate architectural implications; as a junior in an established professional firm, he could not be expected to revolutionize that firm's output. None the less, over the following two years there are

intimations that Mackintosh was able to contribute substantially to some of the office designs – evidence that he was attempting to realize his graphic work architecturally.

At first this evidence appears where one would expect it, as decorative embellishments to otherwise entirely conventional buildings. The first building where this appears to any notable extent is the *Glasgow Herald* building, designed in 1893–4. Here, the organization of the main block is in an entirely ordinary Queen Anne cum Scottish Baronial cum Victorian commercial idiom. Its only noteworthy elements are the pedimented window heads on the top floor, where the Queen Anne detail has begun to melt and flow under the hot breath of Art Nouveau. But it is in the handling of the tower unit that the mind of Mackintosh becomes clearly evident.

During the Victorian period the office block as a building type emerged, and, with the crowding of cities, economic pressures, and the sharp rise in land values, it became necessary to use awkward corner sites, and to fill those sites completely. As a consequence, the architectural device successfully illustrated here became commonplace. This was to place some multi-faceted vertical element, usually an implied tower form, on the awkward angled corner. The device had the double advantage of enabling the architect to 'turn' the corner and compose the remaining façades independently, and to place a major entrance conveniently at the point which was commercially most desirable, yet architecturally most difficult: the exposed corner. In the case of the *Glasgow Herald* building, the tower image is accentuated by incorporating the water storage and services at the top. Mackintosh had commented favourably, during his tour, on the campanile at Siena; he had been much impressed by the dignity of its severe plainness, and by the satisfactory lightening effect created by the gradual increase in the number of openings in the tower as it rose. There can be little doubt that this was very much in his mind as he – and it must have been he – arranged the series of vertical windows in the tower, particularly the top triplet in the plane of the corner entrance. But the tower image, almost an illusion, is really maintained by the tall, slender pilasters rising up the angles. Much of their success is due to the small detail of curving them out from the face of the walls, thus implying continuity with the wall planes, rather than articulating them with a sharp angle. This device – repeated in the small top-storey balconies – became commonplace, not only with Mackintosh, but with many of his English contemporaries during this period.

The crowning stages of the tower are curious, and, although it is easy to see both their Scottish Baronial and Art Nouveau affinities, must be regarded as a 'living fancy' not yet resolved. The strongly articulated ogee roof, however, has a family resemblance to the railway terminus scheme.

In the other buildings of the period to 1894 in which Mackintosh's hand is evident, such as the work for the Glasgow Art Club, the alterations to the 1872 Craigie Hall by Honeyman, and the Canal Bargemen's Institute, the work of Mackintosh is difficult to distinguish with certainty from the direction of John Keppie, and seems to have been restricted principally to decorative details. It is unlikely that he would have been given an entirely free hand with these, and the interest lies chiefly in noting the emergence of Art Nouveau characteristics, and the interconnections with other contemporary buildings of the period.

In 1894 the firm designed a small building, Queen Margaret's Medical College, in which Mackintosh's hand is still more evident. According to the record, it was nominally designed by John Keppie, but it is clear that Mackintosh had a considerable part in the scheme, and may well have been ultimately responsible for its basic conception. For the planning of the building is precisely what would be expected from an admirer of modern Gothic rather than from a Beaux Arts-trained designer such as Keppie. The various spaces, disparate in volume and function, are clustered around a central vestibule which rises through the two floors. Each of these functional elements is expressed as a separate form on the exterior, as is the staircase. Further, the disposition of windows is not according to any

Queen Margaret's Medical College, Glasgow, 1894–5. The exterior is now surrounded with other buildings, and the original interiors totally altered.

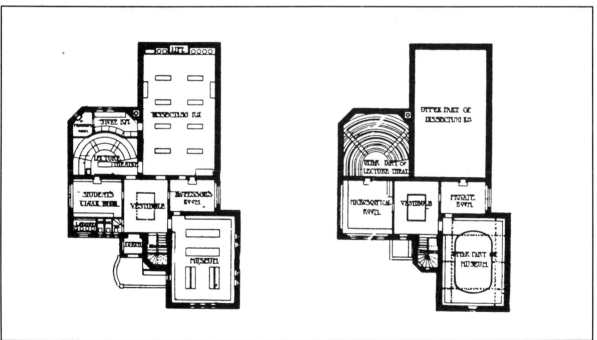

recognizable system of visual composition, but rather as the precise reflection of the pattern of internal spaces. For instance, the two storeys of windows to the left of the main entrance are arranged in size and location to best serve the rooms within, in accordance with the Gothic Revival principles of 'truth' and 'reality'. Similarly, the tall narrow windows serving the staircase tower decrease successively in height to follow faithfully the climbing treads.

The plainness of the walls, the strongly rectangular quality of the masses emphasized by the use of parapets in conjunction with exposed gables, is very reminiscent, and probably not accidentally so, of the sort of work that Leonard Stokes was doing in England. It is clear that, in precept and practice, Mackintosh was thoroughly in accord with the most progressive English work of the time.

But there was another facet of his architectural interest very much in evidence at this time: his love of inventive graphic detail. Inventive it was, but he insisted on its origin being found in Nature. Professor Thomas H. Bryce, the client for this building, recalled Mackintosh peering through his microscope at a segment of a fish's eye, and then drawing the image with great delight. He subsequently returned to the professor, asking to see more, and confessing that the fish-eye motif had proved decoratively useful in a number of applications. It would be difficult, on this basis, to trace the origin of much of the curious ornament that graced his work, but it can be assumed that all of it, no matter how obscurely, had a natural source.

From evidence presented by Roger Billcliffe, including two interior photographs, it now appears not only that Mackintosh was responsible for the design, but that in its double-height museum with surrounding gallery, it anticipates a series of Mackintosh interiors, culminating in the School of Art library. This anticipation lies not only in the basic configuration of the space, but in the use of the structural bones of the gallery as the means of architectural visual elaboration.

Another building, displaying similar character, was the Martyr's Public School, designed about 1895. Here, the disposition of the building's elements is basically symmetrical: a symmetry, however, that is not the result of aesthetic considerations, but of the traditional educational separation of the sexes. Three classroom blocks surround a central hall, and are linked by twin staircases; again, every effort is made to demonstrate this disposition on the exterior of the building. The roof of the staircase, for example, could so easily have been made continuous with that of the adjacent classroom block;

Right Martyrs Public School. Upper storey of the main hall. Mackintosh's preoccupation with the timber truss work, exposed brackets, and rafters, not only continued a Gothic Revival tradition, but evidently owed much to the Japanese. It continued throughout his architectural career.

Below Martyrs Public School, perspective, 1895. The Mackintosh perspective technique whose development is shown in the past three illustrations owed much in its beginning to Sandy McKibbon, who taught in the School of Art.

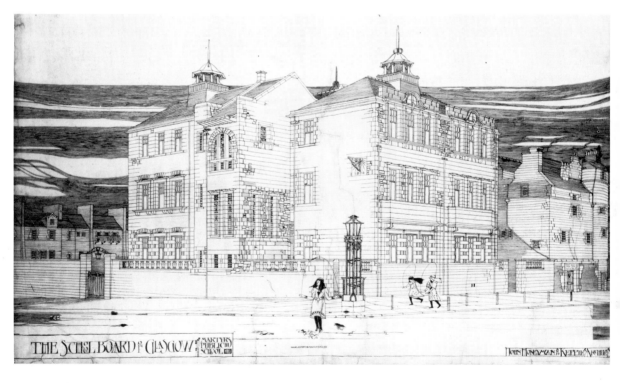

instead, it is articulated by means of a thin line of coping running up the roof slope, and by the cantilevered eave over the large window.

Many of the details of this building are recognizable from the earlier two, such as the vestigial decorative window pediments, and other details which only depart from traditional precedent by the introduction of typical Art Nouveau curves. But there is some fresh departure evident. The cantilevered eaves over the staircase walls are extremely unusual, and forecast a preoccupation that was to characterize all of Mackintosh's subsequent work. This was the creation of novel visual effects by manipulating the physical elements from which the building was constructed, rather than superimposing extraneous decorative elements. This is even more apparent in the interior, with the treatment of the main hall roof trusses, and it may well be that the interest in the jointing and assembly of wooden members grew from Mackintosh's increasing involvement during this time with furniture design. It was, of course, in no way unusual for Victorian architects to engage seriously in the design of furniture, although as the century progressed, the days of the 'great patron' receded, and mass-production determined market values, the opportunities for the architect to control the entire visual environment within their buildings rapidly diminished. Indeed, in 1893 Voysey confessed his own ambivalence to his wallpaper designing activities in a way that clearly reveals the architect's interest in, and frustration with, furniture design. He admitted that, were contemporary furnishings acceptable, he would have no use whatever for patterned

wallpapers, but: 'as most modern furniture is vulgar and bad in every way, elaborate papers of many colours help to disguise its ugliness'.

It was from 1894 onwards that Mackintosh engaged actively in furniture design, although he had, according to Billcliffe, designed a few pieces in the previous year. In 1895 he rented a small studio where he could carry out various craft and decorative commissions in his spare time. The Macdonald sisters had themselves opened a studio in the previous year, on completion of their training at the School of Art, and MacNair, having completed his articles under Honeyman and Keppie, left their employment and set up on his own. The close collaboration of The Four continued, however, and they became the focus for a considerable collection of disciples, emulators and well-wishers.

During 1894 and 1895 Mackintosh designed a number of pieces of furniture for William Davidson, for his home Gladsmuir, in Kilmacolm, and perhaps more importantly for Wells & Guthrie Ltd, a firm of Glasgow decorators. It now appears that his work for Guthrie & Wells was considerably more extensive than had hitherto been assumed. Not only did he design a number of pieces for their catalogue, but prepared decorative stencils, and, according to Michael Donnelly, reporting in the Charles Rennie Mackintosh Society Newsletter No. 25, at least one complete interior.

The furniture and the one evidence of comprehensive interior design, taken together, are instructive. For they indicate quite forcibly the characteristics which were to set Mackintosh apart in his generation, even at this early date. The furniture at this stage tended to be of simple, comparatively severe design, the rigid rectangularity relieved only by the occasional long, taut, sweeping curve that so characterized his graphic work, and by the 'craftwork' strap hinges and fittings. He avoided the use of varnish, using dark brown or green stains. The result, up to this point, was very similar to, but usually more severe than, the simpler products of the English Arts and Crafts school. But there were two basic differences. First, Mackintosh relied primarily on very basic joinery techniques, involving the most straightforward of mortice and tenon jointing, and showed none of the preoccupation of Gimson, the brothers Barnsley, or even Lethaby, with more demanding woodworking techniques, such as exposed dovetailing, decorative splining and veneering. Second, the furnishings in all their comparative severity, began to be carcasses on which to impose the graphic predilections of The Four. These were in the form of beaten metal panels, ironmongery or stencilled fabric, as appropriate. The marriage between themes which were already in latent conflict in the south had begun to appear.

Perhaps even more important than this, certainly more important in understanding Mackintosh's total achievement, was the lifelong preoccupation which shows in the newly discovered Wells & Guthrie interior. It is a design for a library in a Glasgow house, and shows the four interior elevations. It is the first tangible evidence of his determination to create total interiors, even on a domestic scale, which establish, develop and amplify a theme throughout the space and its contained objects.

There is a very real sense in which, at this stage of his development, Mackintosh could have benefited from a closer contact with the rich experimentation, and diverse experience, of his peers in the south. There is no doubt that as his own vision unfolded, he could have offered to them insights which they badly needed. The opportunity seemed to present itself in the Arts and Crafts Exhibition Society exhibition of 1896.

The reputation of the Glasgow designers, and particularly of The Four, was just beginning to trickle beyond the confines of the

Right Glasgow School of Art. Main entrance.

48

Glasgow artistic scene, and they were invited to participate in the 1896 exhibition in London. At that time there were two clearly distinguishable attitudes beginning to emerge among the Arts and Crafts heirs of William Morris. One saw its way out of the contemporary stylistic dilemma by a more disciplined and systematic return to native historic precedent than had been characteristic of Morris and his contemporaries. This impulse was underlaid by an increasing self-consciousness both nationally and professionally; nationally, in the desire to explore and exploit the unique qualities of the English Renaissance, and professionally, in the wish to anchor wildly vacillating architectural taste to a standard of historical scholarship. The other group, of which W. R. Lethaby was the principal figure, saw salvation in the literal interpretation of Morris's definition of art as being *anything* done *well*, and thus, architecturally and decoratively, in the abandonment of any pretence to style of any kind. The vacuum thus left was to be filled with concentration on those matters which are loosely grouped under 'function' – on matters quantitative and measurably qualitative. Thus both groups, for different reasons, bitterly opposed anything that purported to establish a new and precedent-free 'style'. This was particularly so of anything that could be identified with the Aesthetic movement. For the enemy had been clearly defined. William Morris, writing in the 1893 volume of essays produced by the Arts and Crafts Exhibition Society, had observed that there were only two contemporary attitudes to the nature of Art that were really serious – his own, with those of his followers, and that of the Aesthetes.

The anger and chagrin of these earnest folk can be understood when they saw what had been invited to their table. Apart from one relatively innocuous hall settle from Mackintosh, the contribution of The Four was largely posters, with some beaten metal work by the Macdonald sisters and one watercolour, rather badly chosen under the circumstances, by Mackintosh. The benign influence of Burne-Jones could not be seen through the malignant presence of Beardsley – and not just Beardsley, for the distortions accorded the human figure in the Glasgow designers' work were beyond Beardsley, and could not conceivably be reconciled with a due respect for Nature.

Although it was assumed in the past that The Four were not invited to exhibit again, it now appears that they did so at the following exhibition in 1899. But in a real sense the label had already been established. They were seen as Aesthetes. The bonds that should have been forged were not, and on the basis of work which was not properly representative of the direction in which he was really moving, Mackintosh was effectively dismissed by his spiritual peers in the south.

One cannot help wondering what might have been the outcome if Mackintosh had been recognized as the ideological peer that he certainly was by such people as Lethaby, Prior, Stokes or Beresford Pite. It is ironic that it was during this very year that Hermann Muthesius first came to England to study British architecture. One of his principal guides was W. R. Lethaby, and he became wholly familiar with the work of what has subsequently been called the English 'Free School'. But he alone appears to have recognized the talent of Mackintosh, and remained in correspondence with him over the following years.

Left Glasgow School of Art. The west façade showing projecting bay windows. The three long windows flanked by cylinders in niches serve the library.

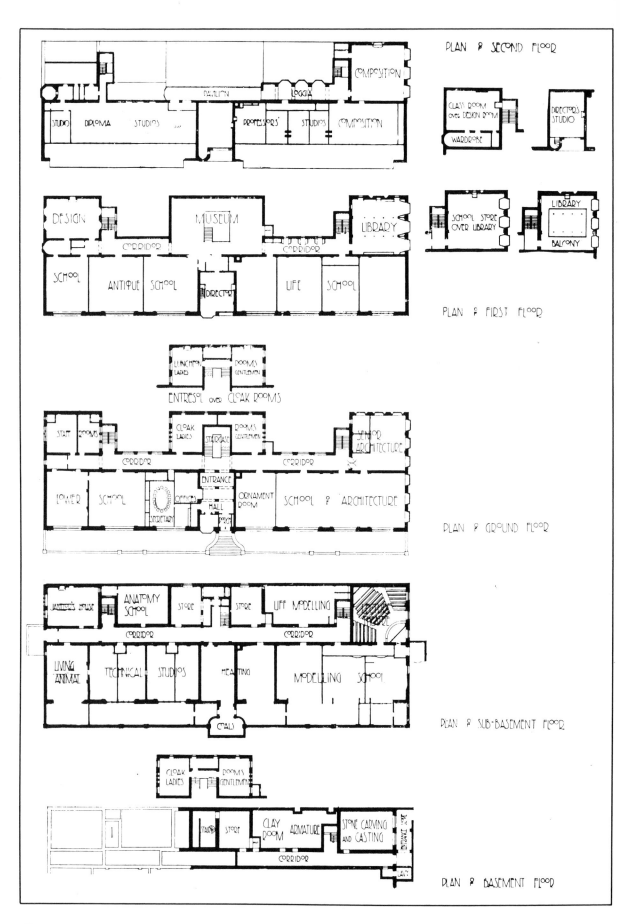

PLAN ℗ SECOND FLOOR

COMPOSITION

STUDIO · DIPLOMA · STUDIOS · · PROFESSORS' · STUDIOS · COMPOSITION

PAVILION · LOGGIA

CLASS ROOM over DESIGN ROOM · DIRECTOR'S STUDIO

WARDROBE

DESIGN · MUSEUM · LIBRARY

CORRIDOR · CORRIDOR

SCHOOL · ANTIQUE · SCHOOL · DIRECTOR · LIFE · SCHOOL

SCHOOL STORE OVER LIBRARY · LIBRARY · BALCONY

PLAN ℗ FIRST FLOOR

LUNCHEON · ROOMS
LADIES · GENTLEMEN

ENTRESOL over CLOAK ROOMS

STAFF · ROOMS · CLOAK · ROOMS · SENIOR ARCHITECTURE
LADIES · GENTLEMEN · STAIRCASE

CORRIDOR · CORRIDOR

LOWER · SCHOOL · OFFICES · ENTRANCE · ORNAMENT ROOM · SCHOOL ℗ ARCHITECTURE
SECRETARY · HALL
PORCH

PLAN ℗ GROUND FLOOR

JANITOR'S HOUSE · ANATOMY SCHOOL · STORE · STORE · LIFE MODELLING

CORRIDOR · CORRIDOR

LIVING ANIMAL · TECHNICAL · STUDIOS · HEATING · MODELLING · SCHOOL

COALS

PLAN ℗ SUB-BASEMENT FLOOR

CLOAK · ROOMS
LADIES · GENTLEMEN

STAIRCASE · STORE · CLAY ROOM · ARMATURE · STONE CARVING and CASTING

CORRIDOR

LAV.

PLAN ℗ BASEMENT FLOOR

50

CHAPTER FOUR:

1896-99

The year 1896 brought several important developments for Mackintosh, apart from the London exhibition.

The first and foremost of these was the limited competition for new premises for the Glasgow School of Art. In 1895 the governors of the School were offered a site, a public appeal was launched, and in February 1896 sufficient capital had been accrued to begin to build. A competition, limited to eight Glasgow architects, later increased to twelve, was initiated with a schedule of accommodation prepared by Newbery. The details of the competition and its history are more than adequately documented in Howarth's book, *Charles Rennie Mackintosh and the Modern Movement*; it is sufficient for this study to note two important aspects of it. First, the amount of money available for the building was £14,000, and second, Newbery's schedule was extremely demanding. It proved, in the end, to be too demanding for the budget, and the competition conditions were amended to bring the two irreconcilables together; the competitors were asked to design a two-stage building, with a first stage to be constructed under the specified sum.

The winners were, as history knows, Honeyman and Keppie. The designer, and he must be admitted as sole designer, was Mackintosh. It is not as surprising as might at first be thought that a young assistant, still a considerable distance from partnership, should have been entrusted with this design. Honeyman and Keppie were an established firm, with a considerable amount of work, and the project was in no way an enviable one. It was not a building to which a great deal of prestige could be attached, and it was, in financial terms, both a small job and relatively demanding. But the second reason may well have been the overriding one. The reins of power in this competition were ultimately in the hands of Francis Newbery. And Newbery was not just Mackintosh's former teacher; he was his friend, patron and admirer. The furore that followed the publication of the winning drawings, unmistakably in Mackintosh's hand, was to be expected. In retrospect, it did not amount to much, and centred primarily on the 'modern' details. And these details in themselves did not amount to much; they are no more than had appeared in earlier productions by Honeyman and Keppie.

The design itself, as submitted in October 1896, is of compelling interest and great importance, for it heralds the arrival of a major architectural talent, and initiated a building which bears in its fabrics the trace of that talent's development over the following thirteen years. It must be emphasized that the design itself was in no way a

Glasgow School of Art. Floor plans.

51

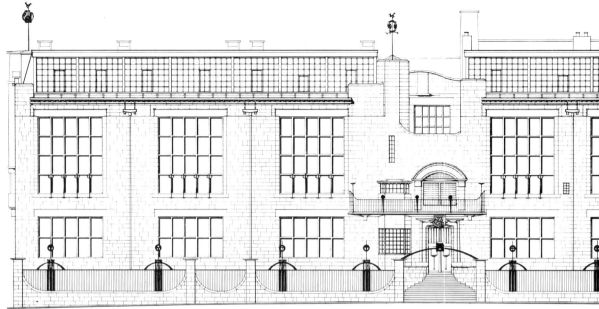

fixed and final thing; to Mackintosh it indicated an intention, and that intention remained in flux, subject to refinement and improvement as the building details emerged, until the physical completion of the fabric.

But what of the first design, of the intention? Initially it was the site that determined the character of the scheme. This was a long, narrow rectangle lying east to west on the south side of the principal access street. There was a tremendous slope from this access street down to

Above Views of the east elevation, with minor later amendments. Many of the forms which recur throughout Mackintosh's work are in evidence here.

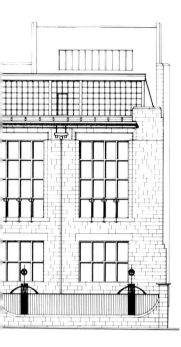

Above Glasgow School of Art. North elevation, from a modern drawing by Hugh C. Ferguson. This drawing shows clearly the casual asymmetry of the building, from an entrance which is in the precise centre of the elevation.

Above, right A view of the north façade.

the southern boundary of the site, which was abutted by a heterogeneous mixture of buildings. The east and west boundaries gave on to secondary streets.

A school of art consists basically of a series of studios connected by corridors and served by various offices: cloakrooms, classrooms and attendant spaces. Studios require north light, and the light they give must be relatively constant, disrupted neither by sun nor shadow. Large windows would be needed for studios of the size that Newbery specified.

It is immediately apparent that on this site the studios would have to be placed on the north – that is, the entrance – face. The depth of the site was such that the major spaces, other than studios, could not be accommodated in the remainder, allowing for the width of a reasonable access corridor to the studios. The result was a plan in the shape of a stubby letter 'E', with a symmetrically placed entrance and staircase, the ends terminating with elements such as the library and lecture rooms, to the south of the studios.

It was, in fact, a simple, logical plan, whose sensible determination was in a virtually complete axial symmetry. And it is here that Mackintosh betrays his British, and uniquely British, antecedents and affections. For the building is almost perversely asymmetrical. It is, further, an asymmetry that cannot be justified pictorially, for the difference in the sizes of the great studio windows, while being readily perceptible on the ground, is not sufficient to create any sense of visual drama, or even progression. They are simply, and under the circumstances almost fanatically, reflective of the varying sizes of the studios within. There can be no doubt whatever that Mackintosh was not only aware of, but committed to, the Gothic Revival principles of design referred to earlier. It would have been the easiest of mathematical exercises to have produced a window size and proportion which would have served the slightly varying size of studio, and yet have produced a uniform exterior bay spacing. This is not to suggest that he was at fault; indeed, the whole school of thought which had led to this decision was the most pregnant with hope in the architectural

53

scene. Mackintosh's commitment to it was in no small way a tribute to his perception, and it contributed, in turn, to his greatness.

The same attitude of mind is evident in the treatment of the entrance bay. Here again, the asymmetry is justified by the logical disposition of the spaces behind. The asymmetrical balance is, of course, much more carefully considered pictorially, as might be expected in view of its prominence, and the fact that it is a single element whose internal visual coherence must be maintained. There was, of course, a good British precedent for this calculated imbalance. Twenty-four years before, Norman Shaw, whose work Mackintosh so much admired, had built the revolutionary New Zealand Chambers in London. It heralded the arrival of the so-called Queen Anne movement in the commercial centre of the city. Comparison

Right New Zealand Chambers, Leadenhall Street, London, by R. Norman Shaw, 1871. The projecting glazed bays were a theme picked up in much work of the next generation (even as far afield as Chicago); in the Mackintosh entrance bay of Glasgow School of Art, 1895–6, they became a dominant element in the second phase of the building.

Left The railings and façade, Glasgow School of Art. The Japanese *mon* theme is clearly evident in the metalwork.

Below The Mary Ward Settlement, Tavistock Place, London, by Dunbar Smith and Cecil Brewer, 1895. The use of the railings and the 'celebratory' screen entrance in front of the main façade have much in common with the Glasgow School of Art.

between this building and the School of Art reveals remarkable similarities of handling, not only in the carefully contrived relationship between the off-set door and small oriel window, but also in the large relationship between the solid entrance bay and the big multi-paned windows on either side.

The visual game that Mackintosh was playing is heightened by the bay spacing of the very prominent front railings. These are precisely symmetrical on either side of the front entrance, indicating, among other things, that the entrance door is in fact in the physical middle of the building. Not only that, but each of the piers, as can be seen in the elevation drawing, arrives at some immediately identifiable relationship with the window spacing behind, with one exception. Thus the determination to let function govern the disposition of the basic elements detracted in no way from attention to visual detail. The actual form of these railings is of interest, for they can be directly related to a building in London designed a year earlier, the Passmore Edwards Settlement, now the Mary Ward Settlement, by Dunbar Smith and Cecil Brewer. In this building there is much the same feeling in the semicircular arch over the principal entrance, and in the thin horizontals of the canopies. The remarkable circular metal plates on the School of Art railings were suggested by Buchanan to be derived from Japanese *mon*, heraldic shields. This has been confirmed by Hiroaki Kimura in his unpublished thesis, where he identifies not only each of the forms, but the specific sources from which each is derived, as illustrated in the books on Japanese art in the School of Art library, acquired in 1887. This interweaving of Japanese sources into British themes was one of the early characteristics which set Mackintosh's work apart from that of his contemporaries, and even when a specific attribution is not evident, the

Japanese feeling, particularly in his white interiors, remained strong.

Mention has been made of the way in which the design of the School of Art, as with all of Mackintosh's later work, was changed and modified as the scheme and the building developed. This was in itself an ideological principle, and characterized most of the work of men who owed allegiance to the teachings of Ruskin and Morris. It owed its origin to the idealized view of medieval society; of a relationship between intelligent craftsmen, each of whom contributed creative skills within an intentional framework provided by the 'master builder'. Faced with the facts of Victorian life, however, the process became subtly modified. Craftsmen, even if skilled, were given neither the facility nor the economic opportunity to be creative, and so a process evolved where the architect himself, on occasion with the participation of superior sculptors or mural painters, engaged in a developing dialogue with the tradesmen on the site, altering and refining details as the concept emerged into a reality. It was, and is, a process which, while giving a great deal of opportunity for second thoughts and refinement as building problems emerge, tends to make the reconciliation between the initial estimate for a building and the final account an impossible exercise.

The changes that occurred in the building of the first section of the school were not major, but taken together they indicate a thoughtful reassessment of every detail of the building fabric. The turret form enclosing the private staircase from the Director's office to his studio was modified and more strongly articulated; small windows were added here and there, and the railings and other ironwork were changed. The entrance door and surround were given a more Art Nouveau form, and the gate pillars received a shallow ironwork arch. One apparent change which is, however, illusory, was the cantilevered roof over the great studio windows. The element which appears on the first elevation as a shallow dentil cornice is in fact this cantilevered roof and its wooden brackets in dead elevation. The low parapet wall shown above this roof line does exist, although it is invisible from the street.

The projecting iron brackets to the studio windows have never escaped attention in any commentary on this building; and whatever attributes critics in their wisdom have given them, they do display one overriding characteristic of Mackintosh's mature decorative enterprise: they are, in the definition by Fergusson with which every Victorian architect was familiar, 'decorated construction' and not 'constructed decoration'. They are used to support window cleaners' planks – an entirely necessary provision – and they provide some bracing to the window mullions. With this functional justification they became the inevitable subjects for Mackintosh's graphic whimsy, and thus the most discussed window brackets in history.

The main staircase and first-floor museum taken together form a fascinating catalogue in timber of Mackintosh's influences and predilections: the modern medievalism of the heavy trusses with their lovingly expressed tenoned and dowelled joints, the stressed Voysey quality of the balusters and newel posts, and the Japanese twinned beams projecting and gripping the newels. Withal, it possesses a remarkable unity, and presages a developing preoccupation with space and its manipulation.

Another more prosaic but equally revealing aspect of the building deserves attention. It incorporates a fully integrated, and by all

Left Glasgow School of Art. Brackets to the studio windows on the north façade.

Left Glasgow School of Art. The main staircase from ground level.

Right Glasgow School of Art. The Museum, and *Below* roof trusses supporting the Museum roof light.

Above A detail of the air plenum duct in the sub-basement. The pipework is the result of later alterations.

Left The main staircase rising to the first floor.

reports most effective, plenum system of heating and ventilation. Under the central corridors at sub-basement level runs a warm-air duct. It is, for most of its length, some six feet high and the full width of the corridors above, and was served by a large fan-room adjacent to the boiler room. Large fresh-air grilles were located beside and below the main entrance, and the main duct fed vertical branches built into the corridor walls which in turn opened into the studios through grilles. The system was extremely carefully considered in relation to the building design; its abandonment some years ago and the substitution of the usual unconsidered jungle of pipes is inexplicable. The system as originally installed was not revolutionary for its time, contrary to some belief; but it did require a high degree of integration with the architectural layout in early stages of planning. And its final complete unobtrusiveness in the building speaks highly of the architect's concern for the environment, and not just the visual picture he was creating.

Of the rooms finished in the 1897–9 phase of the School building, two in particular indicate the direction in which Mackintosh's style was moving. The room originally used as a boardroom, in the east wing, is an airy, simple space, beautifully lit by two tall windows in each of the east and west walls. The quality of the light is consciously enhanced by pushing the windows out into bays and providing white painted, curving 'cheeks' as reflective surfaces. The large steel beams spanning the ceiling are exposed and painted white, doubtless an economy measure, but one which was obviously happily accepted, and their position clearly determines the location and size of the elegant fireplace surround.

Even more indicative of certain development is the Director's office. It is another white room, with painted panelling. But here the panelling is carried uniformly around the room, tying together door heads, fireplace surround, cupboard doors, staircase opening, and window rail. It sharply delineates the wall from what is to be read as the ceiling. In this room, as in most of his future rooms, the ceiling is modelled in such a way as to emphasize the function of certain areas. For instance, the recess into the window bay, clearly a writing or study space, is marked by a shallow arch at a considerably lower lever than the general ceiling. It springs, in fact, from the top of the dado, and creates a significant change in scale within the total space. In this

Right Chair, 1902. This chair, in white painted oak, was exhibited in Turin in 1902, and some of this type appear to have been made for Fritz Wärndorfer for his music salon.

This page Glasgow School of Art. The original Board Room in the East Wing. This was used as a studio from the beginning, due to lack of space. The furniture shown here was an assembly of pieces from various sources on display in the 1960s.

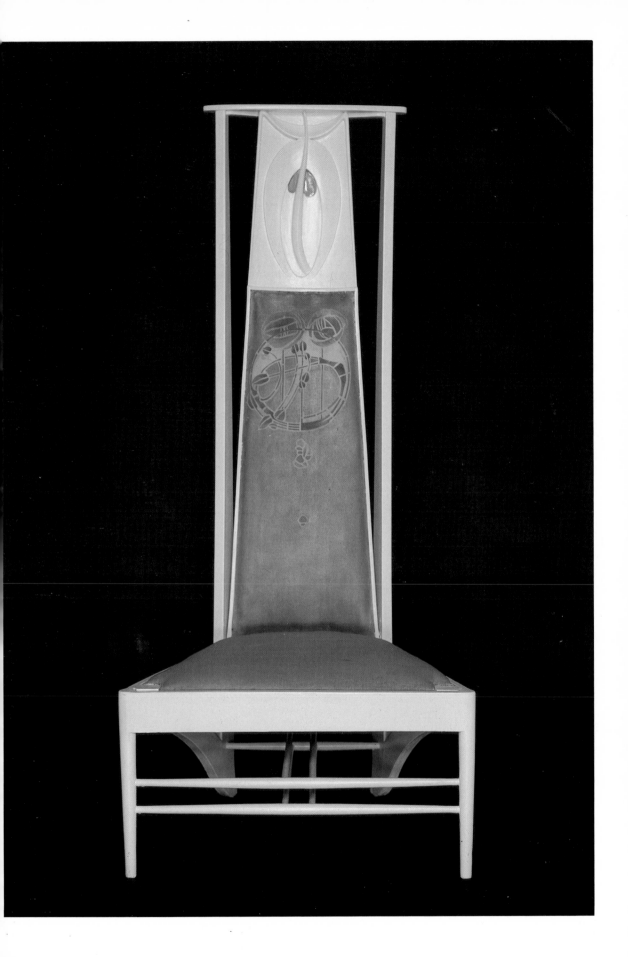

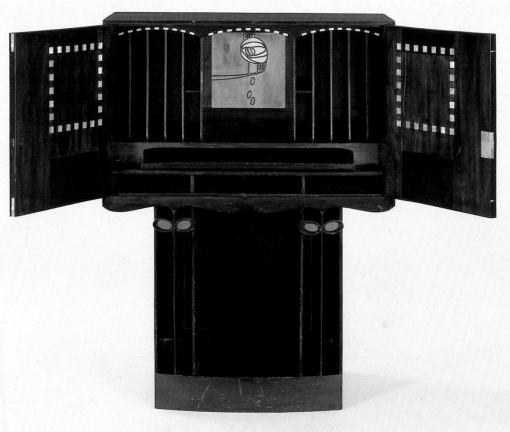

Left, above Design for stencilled mural decoration, Buchanan Street Tea Rooms, Glasgow, 1896.

Left, below Writing cabinet, 1904. This was Mackintosh's own cabinet, built as a duplicate of one designed for Walter W. Blackie at Hill House.

Below Glasgow School of Art. The Director's Room. The furniture has been assembled from other sources, in particular the large chair originally designed for the Willow Tea Rooms' order desk in 1904.

room two different levels of design interest are fused together: levels which all too frequently remain dissociated. The first is the interest which locates a room and determines its principal elements such as windows and doors; the second, that which then analyses the disparate activities that take place within that room, providing for them by means of fittings and furnishings. What is beginning to be apparent here, and was to become even more marked, is their interaction; for instance, the small-scale consideration that provided a suitable size and situation for the writing recess early enough in the design process for it to appear as an exterior element on the face of the building.

The opportunity to explore problems of interior design on a large scale came in the year of the School of Art competition, with Mackintosh's introduction to Miss Catherine Cranston. Miss Cranston was one of that special breed of women who rise to prominence in every generation, combining a shrewd and precise business acumen with an equally precise taste and flair for the dramatic. With her father's help, and subsequently that of her husband, she established herself in the tea-room business. This was a particularly Glaswegian phenomenon of the turn of the century, an enthusiasm for non-

Right The Buchanan Street Tea Room.

Below The Peacock. Study for mural decoration in Miss Cranston's Buchanan Street Tea Room, Glasgow, 1897–8.

alcoholic places of refreshment that combined the facilities of gentlemen's midday clubs with the gentilities of ladies' afternoon tea. In a remarkably short space of time Glasgow became served with a very high standard of public catering. When Mackintosh met Miss Cranston, she was already well established as a tea-room proprietress, but was just on the threshold of a remarkable programme of expansion.

At the time of their meeting, Miss Cranston had two premises undergoing structural and decorative preparation for catering, in Buchanan Street and Argyle Street. Over the following two years Mackintosh executed work for both of these, in conjunction with other designers, notably George Walton.

These establishments were rather more extensive than is suggested by the name. They included tea rooms, luncheon rooms for each sex, general luncheon rooms, dinner rooms, billiards rooms, and smoking rooms. They provided the designers with opportunities for whimsy and decorative extravagance not normally acceptable in ordinary architectural commissions.

It is not therefore surprising that in the Buchanan Street premises, to which Mackintosh contributed only murals in association with Walton's furniture, he simply transcribed his highly effective poster technique in terms of bold stencilled patterns. But even with these highly personalized forms, his allegiance to Arts and Crafts principles is evident. Voysey, in the interview recorded in the first issue of *The Studio*, had emphasized the necessity to show the ties in

ANNAN.16106

stencilled patterns – in other words, the technique must be clearly evident as 'honest' design, and there must be no attempt to create the illusion of conventional painting. It is evident that Mackintosh consciously adhered to this – the pattern of the ties is not only apparent but is organized to provide an additional rhythm in the design.

In the following project, the Argyle Street Tea Rooms, Mackintosh's contribution was again a limited one, this time to the movable furniture. In this furniture many typical Mackintosh forms can be seen emerging. Like his work in other fields, it shows the curious blending of Arts and Crafts traditional forms with the severely linear qualities of the Godwin-Aesthetic school. But there can be seen too his sometimes quixotic delight in pursuing functional considerations to inventive ends. The buttock-shaped recesses in the wooden stool surfaces would certainly require a posterior commitment of unreasonable accuracy.

These two small projects laid the foundation for a continuing collaboration which was to extend over the next twenty years, and was to provide Mackintosh with one of the most important of the tragically small range of opportunities that came his way.

During the time that he was engaged on these first tea-room projects, Mackintosh was, of course, fully occupied in the office. He began his work on a design for a church at Queen's Cross, Glasgow,

Left and *Right* Views of Queen's Cross Church, Glasgow, 1897–99. Although the engaged turret was typical of many Somerset, and other, medieval parish churches, the dramatic battering of the tower was not, and the compressed articulation of the main elements to the street, including the massive flying buttress, was much more characteristic of the late Gothic Revival precedents, beginning with All Saints, Margaret Street.

immediately after finishing the School of Art competition drawings. This was a project of considerable importance, not only for its own intrinsic interest, but as a revealing indication of his allegiance to tradition. For a church presented no startlingly new functional demands, although its forms and fabric were steeped in meaningful symbolism and association; this was no less true, although in certain symbolic respects more *negatively* true, for the Church of Scotland than for the Church of England.

The most notable characteristic of this church, then, is its traditional handling. This is not to say that it was not, in contemporary

Left Queen's Cross Church. A side aisle. The predilection for exposed structure continued to be an established Mackintosh theme, and the decorative gallery pendants anticipate very clearly an element of his later, more famous interiors.

Below Queen's Cross Church. The nave. This interior – mixing the traditional with the new, the rich with the raw, the iconographic with the functional – is typical of the paradox that gripped Mackintosh's generation, and that remains an issue today.

terms, modern, but it is the modernity of those who placed a high value on past ways, the modernity of Bodley, of Bentley, Sedding and Stokes. Howarth's discovery of the source for the tower and engaged turret in a sketch of Merriot Church, Somerset, is of interest in this regard, but it is also worth noting how Mackintosh justified, or at least excused, the use of that particular form by the internal planning of the gallery staircase. Of course, in its details the church became the subject of Mackintosh's personal inventiveness; but even here, it was little further removed from historical precedent than, say, Stokes' Church of St Clare at Sefton Park, Liverpool, of 1888–90; in both there is a clear dependence on the precedent of Bodley and Sedding. It is worth noting, too, how essentially close the handling is with the east end of the School of Art, even to the predilection with the engaged octagonal form. Of course the Art School was plainer, but this was the product of propriety and economy, not of 'modernity'. The interior details of the church give a true picture of what was meant then by 'modernity'. The great steel roof ties, frankly exposed with their pattern of rivets, owe little to tradition – but they are in the same place as, and fulfil the same role as, the great adzed timbers of a medieval roof. And every other element, even to the 'east' window, although answering tradition, is, on inspection, novel in form and detail. Certain of the details here, notably the gallery balustrading with its posts and pendants, recur

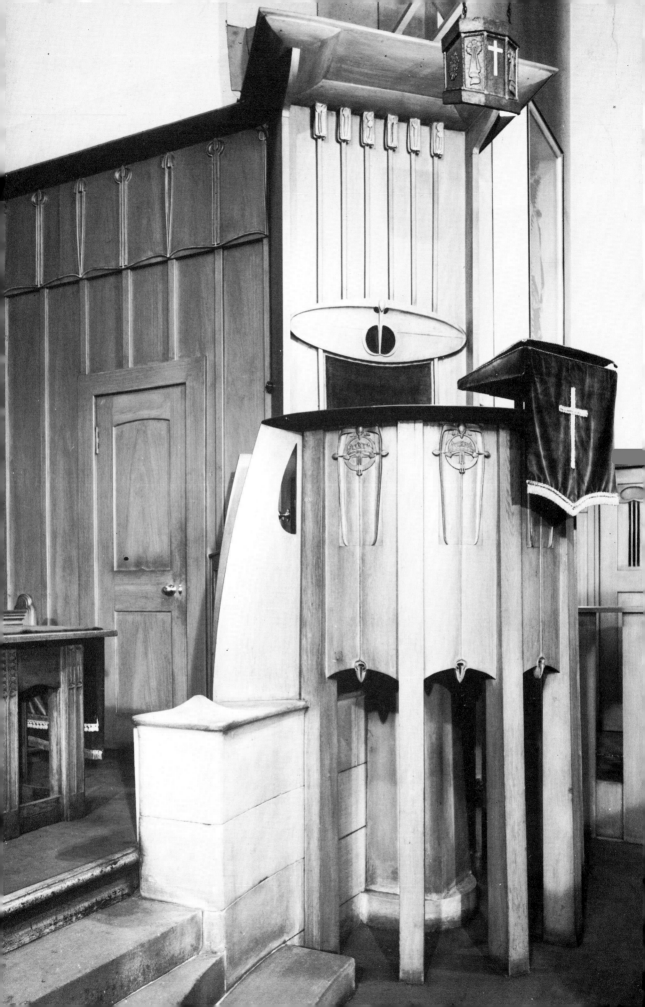

Queen's Cross Church. *Left* The
pulpit, and *Right* a detail of its
panelling. These provide an
indication of the elaboration of
traditional building materials and
methods, as contrasted with the
raw 'bones' of the structure. In
their strong rectilinear control they
also anticipate the last phase of his
architectural manner.

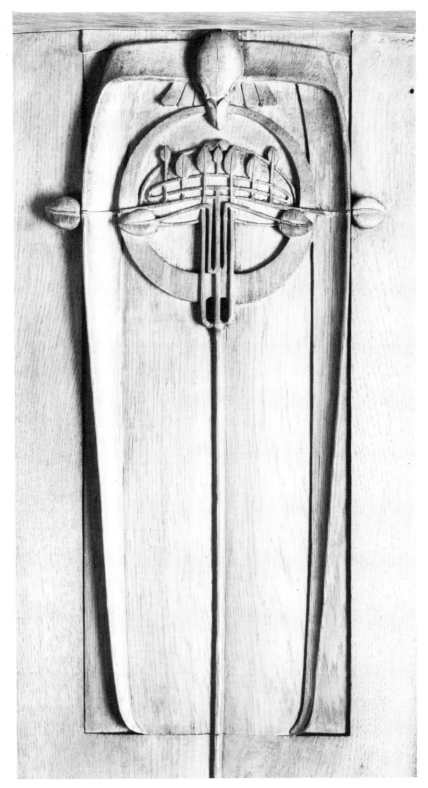

time and again, with variations, through Mackintosh's later designs –
as in the interior details for the *Haus eines Kunstfreundes*, the Oak
Room for Miss Cranston, and finally the library of the School of Art.

One other point is deserving of notice here. Critics past and
present of the graphic innovations of the Macdonald sisters, Mac-
Nair and Mackintosh have accused them of a conscious wish to

outrage, and even of possessing a tinge of moral decadence. There can be no doubt that much of this feeling can be directly attributed to its association in the minds of the critics with the whole Oscar Wilde-Aubrey Beardsley ethos; it is perfectly clear that The Four saw no such sinister symbolism in their own work. They were developing what they felt to be a meaningful iconography for a new age out of the forms of the past, and Mackintosh could use these writhing, curiously organic forms for the tracery of a church window with a sense of perfect propriety.

This attitude was realized with some surprise by Gleeson White, the editor of *The Studio*, in 1897. His was the only voice publicly raised in support of the Glasgow designers during the Arts and Crafts exhibition of 1896, and he subsequently visited the group to investigate their work further. The result was a pair of articles in *The Studio* during 1897, entitled 'Some Glasgow Designers and their Work'. Not only was White astonished at the youth and 'wholesomeness' of the designers, but at the absence of a revolutionary attitude. Of the Macdonald sisters he said: 'With a delightfully innocent air these two sisters disclaim any attempt to set precedent at defiance. . . .' What White did not perhaps realize was that the sisters retained through their lives serious religious convictions, and they were quite as

Craigie Hall, possibly 1892–4. If Mackintosh was involved in this project, it must have been in the early stages of the alterations. The swirling, dynamic decorative features remain within a much earlier, more typically Victorian context.

prepared to use their art to depict the Annunciation and the Nativity as Beardsley was to illustrate the *Lysistrata* of Aristophanes.

These articles by Gleeson White were the only significant benefits accrued by the 1896 London exhibition. *The Studio* was avidly read on the Continent, and as a result Alexander Koch of Darmstadt published an article on the Glasgow designers in *Dekorative Kunst*, in November 1898. Thus began an appreciation that was to sustain the designers and stimulate them through many years of apathy at home.

During this period in the office Mackintosh was engaged in a minor capacity on a number of commissions under the direction of the partners. It is difficult to identify these from the surviving office records, and there may be identifiable projects extant which may yet come to light. Of those which have emerged in recent years, one at least is of particular interest. Craigie Hall was designed by John Honeyman in 1872, and the firm undertook revisions to the house on two occasions during the 1890s. It is apparent that Mackintosh was involved in decorative designs for the hall and library, but the most important evidence is from the music room, which is undeniably his. A very splendid organ case, dated 1897, shows the growing certainty of his handling, and it anticipates almost exactly a project which although never built remains one of the most celebrated of his early projects. It is the organ case shown in the drawings of the concert hall for the Glasgow Exhibition.

Craigie Hall. The Organ Case, Music Room, 1897. Here the developing Mackintosh idiom, as in Queen's Cross Church, is much more apparent and assured.

In 1898 a competition was held for the design of an international exhibition to be held in Glasgow in 1901. Honeyman and Keppie submitted three schemes, of which one was by Mackintosh. Although unsuccessful in the competition, his design is of interest in showing his developing style applied to a new problem. Although relatively conventional in plan and even in the disposition of the elements, the forms used are probably more radical than any he used in his architecture before or after. It is entirely likely that the temporary nature of exhibition building made Mackintosh feel justified in abandoning his reliance on 'tradition' to an unusual degree – it was not, perhaps, entirely 'serious' building. The quality generated, however, is extremely gay and appropriate, and there is a certainty and verve about the handling that makes this work, among those who were attempting to be 'modern', astonishingly unusual. This quality is particularly apparent in the design of the concert hall, although knowing Mackintosh's immense capacity for re-orienting and transforming borrowings, it may well owe something of its form, and the forms of the buttresses, to the roof domes then being constructed on Bentley's Westminster Cathedral.

In the meantime, The Four disbanded. Herbert MacNair accepted a post as Instructor in Decorative Design at Liverpool University in 1898, and the following year married Frances Macdonald. Their departure cannot be considered in any sense a handicap to Mackintosh's development, for although he and MacNair were close friends, there was no doubt as to who was the prime mover in the artistic relationship. MacNair never undertook any architectural work, and his subsequent decorative efforts did not move significantly beyond his youthful Glasgow level. The difference between the men was noted by Augustus John, who was a contemporary of MacNair's at Liverpool, and subsequently friendly with Mackintosh in Chelsea. For MacNair he had little but scorn, for Mackintosh a considerable respect.

Perspective drawing of the Glasgow International Exhibition of 1901. One of the schemes submitted by Honeyman & Keppie for the competition held in 1898.

76

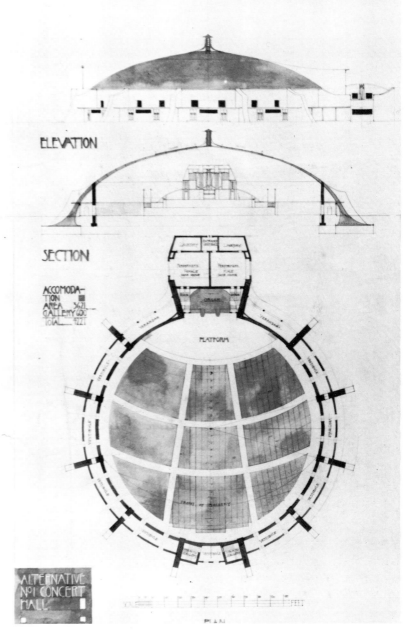

Above Entrance elevation, Industrial Hall, and *Right* Alternative No. 1 for a Concert Hall in the Glasgow International Exhibition.

These three drawings, taken together, illustrate the prevailing ambivalence of the age and indeed of the architect. The forms of the first two drawings are 'developed Gothic', modified by the Ecole des Beaux Arts, stripped of their decorative detail and affirming the decorative iconography of their time. The Concert Hall drawing, although almost feasible at that time, anticipates the structural experiments of Felix Candela and Pier Luigi Nervi by half a century.

As the century drew to an end, and Mackintosh moved into his thirties, the prospect was fair. He had a position of some seniority in the firm, and was being given a free hand with some interesting building projects. His private practice was beginning to develop, and the decorative commissions he had executed received publicity disproportionate to their size. Life was very full, and though the demands were beginning to be heavy, his energy and enthusiasm were equal to the challenge. He had always been intense and determined; but the intensity, in these happy circumstances, could find expression in high enthusiasm, and the determination was couched in a very real personal charm.

CHAPTER FIVE:

1899-1901

The development of the detached family house during the latter nineteenth century was the one area of architectural effort above all others in which British architects were universally deemed to have excelled. This was so much so that the interest in British domestic architecture, both at home and abroad, became almost obsessional. From the 1890s to the outbreak of the First World War domestic and foreign journals were filled with plans and cloying little perspectives, competitions for designs for non-existent clients on non-existent sites were organized, and, almost obscured by the honeysuckle and the thatch, a considerable body of meritorious work was actually achieved. Riding the crest of this wave of popularity, and no doubt slightly bewildered by it, was C. F. A. Voysey. With its sheer innocent directness, his work created an imagery which, almost by accident, won the affection of an age sated with eclectic excess. Similarly popular, and for similar reasons, were the quaint domestic exercises of Hugh Mackay Baillie Scott; although his houses, with their adzed beams, cosy ingles and childlike stencilled patterns had little of the cool clarity of Voysey, the appeal to traditional values and the self-conscious informality of both were much the same.

In 1899 Mackintosh received his first independent commission for a house (excluding an unimportant pair of houses built for his uncle in 1890). The client was William Davidson, for whom he had already carried out some minor decorative work. Davidson was a discerning patron of the arts, and an admirer of Mackintosh's work, so the architect found himself in an ideal situation for exploring his convictions with the full sympathy of his client.

The site is located high on a south-sloping hillside on the outskirts of the town of Kilmacolm. It has a panoramic view of rolling, pastoral landscape, and is served by a road running along the northern border. The house is set on a slight plateau somewhat below the level of the road and separated from it by a small courtyard; from the south front the garden swings away down a steep slope of terraced planting to an enclosing garden wall below.

The appearance of Windyhill is curiously paradoxical; it combines the traditional and the unprecedented, the casual and the precise, the bleak and the picturesque. The materials and their constructional assembly are all entirely traditional, conforming with considerable technical awareness to the best accepted practice. The structure is of whinstone finished with brick around windows and doors for easy working; the whole, including the returns around door and window openings, is then rough-cast – the economical and effective ancient

Left Windyhill, Kilmacolm, 1899–1901. *Top* The north façade. *Bottom* The south façade. The starkness of these exteriors, particularly of the south façade, is that of traditional Scottish housing, not a conscious desire to be modern.

Scottish response to rains that fall horizontally as often as vertically. In accordance with the same precedent, the walls rise beyond and protect the gable ends of the roofs, which are finished with slate.

As one would expect by now, the insistence that elements be disposed by function and not by appearance is quite evident, but at Windyhill there is an odd compulsiveness about it, as when the roof guttering is allowed to bisect the dormer windows on the north face, when windows are not only misaligned in position and size, but their very panes vary from one to the next. This in itself is not unusual; it is an expression of the conscious gaucheness, the anti-pretty attitude that had as its chief historical exponents William Butterfield and Philip Webb. What *is* unusual is that together with this can be seen Mackintosh the post-traditionalist, the formal graphic composer at work, as in the artful lapping planes of the entrance porch element and the stair tower, the thin, flat planes of the nursery alcove and the south bay window. The appearance of irresolution is further heightened by the self-consciously artful garden wall. This, with its rubble texture, patches of dressed coping, its curves and swoops along the boundaries, even its casual embrace of an ancient bothy, is a country dance by a ballerina, a faintly uncomfortable parody.

But what of the plan that generates such ambivalence? It is clear, direct, and eminently workable. It is almost certainly derived from

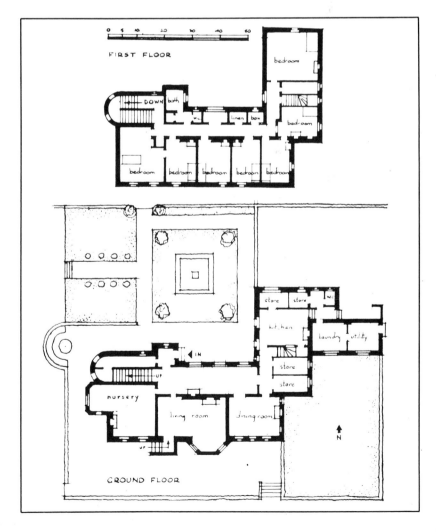

Left Windyhill, Kilmacolm. The main entrance. The casual treatment of this entrance, with its informal conjunction of walls, roofs, windows and door is typical. *Right* Windyhill Plans. The clear and ordered plans explain, in the best Gothic Revival manner, the massing and articulation of the exterior. In general disposition it reflects Lethaby's The Hurst (*see* overleaf), in detail it anticipates Mackintosh's next major domestic project, Hill House.

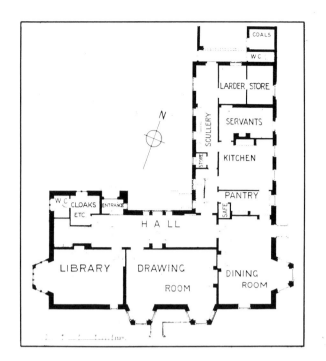

a design by Lethaby for The Hurst at Sutton Coldfield of 1893. Although Mackintosh has rotated the dining room through ninety degrees and disposed the service wing slightly differently, the generic similarity is striking, even to the inclusion of a single bay (in place of Lethaby's two) on the south face of the drawing room. As if this were not enough, Mackintosh has used an identical square pond, complete with ornamental trees, from the Lethaby garden, relocating it on the north face of the house. The similarity ends there, but it was a plan type to which Mackintosh returned with his later and larger Hill House. Again, as might be expected, it is characterized not only by the thoughtful, functional relationship of rooms one to

The Hurst, Sutton Coldfield, by W. R. Lethaby, 1893.
Above, left Ground floor plan.
Above, right Part of the gardens to the south west. *Below* A view from the south east. Although there is little external architectural similarity with Windyhill, the similarity in planning is clearly more than a coincidence. This is reinforced by Mackintosh's adoption of the square garden pool with its four trees for the north-facing court of Windyhill.

Right Windyhill. Window seats in the bedroom corridor. This delightful architectural diversion anticipates the famous seating bays in the first floor corridor of the west wing of the Glasgow School of Art.

Left Windyhill. Principal stair landing.
Right The dining room, and *Below* the principal bedroom, as recently restored.

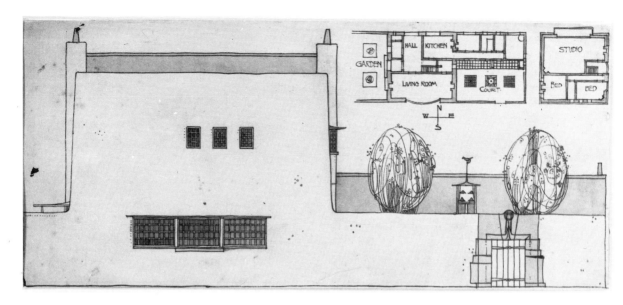

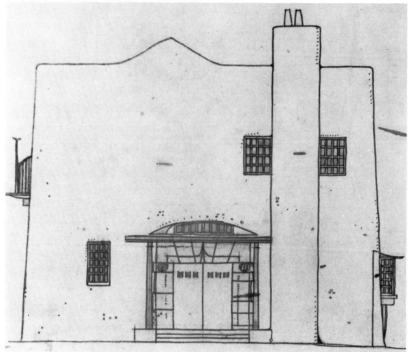

A Country Cottage for an Artist, 1901. *Above* South elevation and plans, and *Left* the west (garden) elevation. *Above, right* The north elevation.

the other, but also that consideration of the precise proportions of the placing of doors, windows and fireplaces that betrays Mackintosh's microscopic concern with details of living. This concern, finally expressed by the carefully detailed built-in fittings, and such whimsically attractive elements as the window alcove in the upper-floor corridor, produces a sense of resolution that is as marked internally as it is absent without. It is, by any standard, a notable house. In the context of Mackintosh's development it is pregnant with possibilities, a clear indication of the direction in which he was to move.

There are two small designs dating from 1901, the year in which construction of Windyhill was completed, which almost suggest that Mackintosh was exploring in the abstract the problems raised by Windyhill. A town house and a country cottage 'for the artist' were the subjects, and they form a related pair. While they are only sketch

designs, with no indication of construction or detail, they are manifestly intended to be read as much the same combination of materials as found at Windyhill. The plans are simple in the extreme and, while adequate, are essentially of interest only in the way they determine the exterior of the buildings. These are exterior studies, exercises in pictorial architecture. Although the plans still determine the exterior, and, as far as can be determined, the rooms are properly served by their windows, the elevations are carefully and precisely controlled. The accomplished graphic artist is now very much in evidence, and if the elevations owe something to Voysey, and in turn to the artful imbalance of Norman Shaw, they are none the less original and highly personal. They do contain affectations, however, that characterize none of his executed work: for instance, the wilful line of the parapet in the country cottage, that pays scant heed to the actual roof line, and would have been not only expensive to build but technically irresponsible. But the importance of these little exercises is that they show the transfer of his graphic skill to an area not yet mastered.

In the same year, Mackintosh produced another design which, although also unexecuted, demonstrated far more dramatically his growing architectural certainty. The *Zeitschrift für Innendekoration* sponsored an international competition for the design of a *Haus eines Kunstfreundes* (an art lover's house).

Over the previous three years, Mackintosh had been engaged in several projects of interior design, as well as furnishing commissions, in which the white interiors for which he became famous began to be seen. Here, suddenly, the resolution of the architectural qualities of Windyhill and the decorative qualities emerging in his interior work came together.

A first prize was not awarded. Baillie Scott was awarded second prize, and Mackintosh was requested to submit further drawings to comply with certain submission requirements. He was then awarded a special prize. Clearly, the impact of his scheme was substantial.

The scheme by Baillie Scott disported itself quaintly around an axial symmetry in ranks of conical turrets, rounded gables, chimney stacks and calculated inconsistencies. It combined all that was

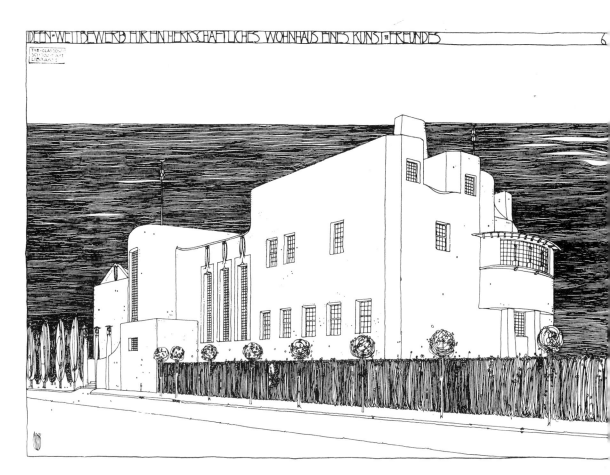

IDEEN·WETTBEWERB·FÜR·EIN·HERRSCHAFTLICHES·WOHNHAUS·EINES·KUNST·FREUNDES   2

OST : WEST

Haus Eines Kunstfreundes. Above
Perspective from the north west,
and *Below* the west elevation.

*Right, above Haus Eines
Kunstfreundes.* The nursery
(labelled *Kinder.Spiel.Zimmer* on
the plan). There are certain minor
inconsistencies between this
perspective and the published
plan.

Right, below Hill House,
Helensburgh. Bay window seat in
the drawing room, as recently
restored.

Overleaf
Left Hill House, from the south
east. The door at the base of the
engaged turret is a recent addition.

implausible about the Arts and Crafts image, and with its institu-
tionalized medieval fantasy lost both the practical sense and the
simple directness of that movement.

The Mackintosh scheme stands out in startling contrast. Its roots,
to be sure, are in traditional building methods, but once this is
acknowledged it can be forgotten, for the way in which these
traditional materials are used generates a quality which is quite new.
The intimation of the forms used was evident in Windyhill, and they
were obviously explored in the two small designs, but what was

88

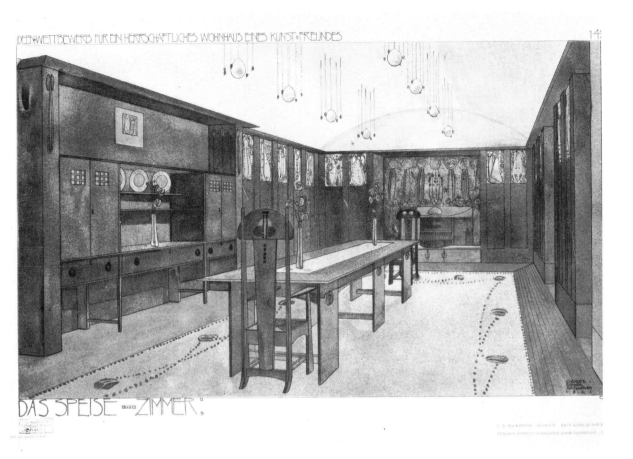

DAS SPEISE = ZIMMER.

Haus Eines Kunstfreundes.
Above The dining room
perspective, and *Right* the plans.

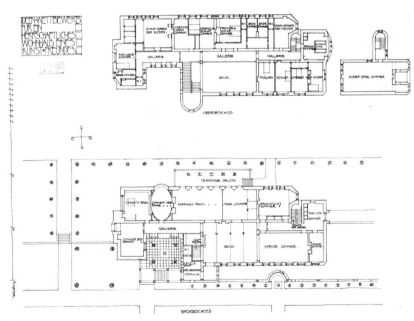

Previous page Hill House,
Helensburgh. Entrance Hall
looking towards the main entrance
and principal staircase.

Left, top Drawing room fireplace,
as recently restored.
Left, bottom Guest bedroom,
showing in foreground the
washstand with decoration almost
anticipating Mondrian.

irresolute in the executed building, and was in danger of degenerating into too-pretty whimsy in the small schemes, is now resolved with clarity and dignity.

In this scheme many threads are drawn together, all of which existed in the work of Mackintosh's British predecessors and contemporaries, but which had never before been combined with such expertise. The plan arrangements and their conformity with structural logic are worthy of Philip Webb; they are as accomplished as the work of Norman Shaw, without his dependence on structural gymnastics for their realization. The elevations are as studied, in their relation of solid and void, of rhythm and accent, as those of Shaw, and yet the features of which they are composed serve the related internal spaces precisely and accurately. The simplicity and elimination of extraneous detail are derived from Voysey, and yet there is neither Voysey's blandness nor his prettiness. There is as much interest in complex internal space as in Baillie Scott – who was, incidentally, the chief exponent of the 'open plan' – without losing for a moment the control of formal relationships. And finally, the whole composition, inside and out, is firmly bonded and stamped with Mackintosh's fully developed personal graphic vocabulary. It is architectural art of a very high order indeed, and in its urban elegance and inventiveness is readily comparable with the innovations of that other earlier Scot, Robert Adam.

But it remained to be proved whether the marvellous virtuosity of the *Haus eines Kunstfreundes* could be produced in a real building, on a real site and, most inhibiting of all, for a real client.

In 1902 Walter Blackie, a publisher, was put in touch with Mackintosh by Talwin Morris, a close friend of the architect, who had been associated with him in his graphic enterprises and was now art manager for Blackie's firm. Blackie, having seen Windyhill, offered Mackintosh the commission for a new house, to be built in the town of Helensburgh. Mackintosh naturally accepted, with the unusual but significant insistence that he must spend some time with the family before actually beginning to design on their behalf.

The site is again on a south-sloping hillside overlooking the town and with a splendid view of the Firth of Clyde. It is a much gentler slope than that at Kilmacolm, and the approach road lies to the west, rather than to the north. The general disposition of the plan is much the same as that of Windyhill, although this house, Hill House as it was named, is noticeably larger, and, in deference to the approach, the main entrance is situated on the end of the building rather than on one of its major faces. The family likeness with Kilmacolm is, moreover, not confined to its plan dispositions. The external materials are also much the same – although the walling material is a local sandstone rather than whin, in accordance with estate requirements – and their detailing and disposition are in the same vein. The stairwell, standing at right-angles to the main axis of the building in the manner of the *Haus eines Kunstfreundes*, is treated in the same way as both its predecessors. The windows, dormers, chimneys and gables all betray their provenance.

But there are significant external differences from both earlier houses. While clearly the externals are disposed according to internal demands, there is much more assured control, particularly on the principal faces, than in the Windyhill scheme. Even in the north courtyard, where the complex massing and variegated planning create external demands difficult of resolution, there is more conscious order than on its simpler predecessor at Windyhill. And on the other faces, the distribution of elements is as careful, in its own way, as in the *Haus eines Kunstfreundes*. But it is different from the competition scheme as well. It is less urbane, and more overtly Scottish. There is no doubt that in both respects this was intended.

Hill House, Helensburgh. *Above*
The view from the south west, and
Right the west (entrance)
elevation.

Mackintosh's use of 'history', if his casual references in this building and Windyhill to the Scottish Baronial idiom can so be called, are almost classic examples of their time. The great fondness he expressed in his 1891 paper for his native tradition was characteristic of a similar interest generally among architects who specifically wished to produce something 'modern' for their own time. And it is notable that the historical periods on which all these British architects focused their interest and affection were what might be called 'transitional' periods when flux and change were evident, when the collar of style was worn loosely over the demands of changing function and building methods: thus the vogue for Queen Anne, modern Gothic – very late and very flat –, Jacobean and Elizabethan, and of course Scottish Baronial. The architects used these styles in a way that might show sympathy without subservience, courtesy without constraint. Thus could the architect, it was hoped, find the sense of direction he so desperately needed, and establish continuity with the past and the existing environment, without in any sense being bound by it.

Mackintosh's commitment to this principle is clear, both from his writing and from the buildings themselves. Hill House and Windyhill are unmistakably heirs of the Scottish Baronial idiom, without

Hill House, Helensburgh. *Below* The entrance gates from the west. *Right* The south-east corner showing the engaged turret, with a garden hut in the foreground. Here the indigenous tradition of two hundred years is most strongly felt.

possessing any single feature that has a direct precedent. The
elements that are most clearly derivative are such things as the small
corner stair tower in the re-entrant angle of the two main wings in
Hill House, yet this is a gesture in kind, not in imitation.

The interior of Hill House is further evidence of progression.
Based on Windyhill, it is larger and more complex. The plan is also,
at first glance, less clear. In fact it is set out with consummate skill,
and the apparent lack of clarity is due to the development that has
taken place in Mackintosh's treatment of the individual rooms. In
this respect the two most notable rooms are the drawing room and the
main bedroom. Looking at them first in plan, one is struck by the
irregularity of outline which may suggest irresolution. In fact the
opposite is true. The drawing room contains two large recesses. One
of these is a bay projecting out of the south face of the building, rather
like the Windyhill prototype, but larger and more sharply delin-
eated. It contains a built-in seat and two doors leading to the garden.
The concentration of light from the expanse of glass is in notable
contrast to the fireplace end, the 'winter' end of the room, which is
served by a single, smaller window. The other major recess was
designed to receive a studio piano or to serve as an informal stage for
the small theatrical performances in which the younger members of
the family liked to engage. There is a nominal cornice or picture rail

Hill House, Helensburgh. The
east wall of the guest bedroom
with fitted wardrobes, seat and
fireplace. This room is designed on
a modest domestic scale, which
obscures how tiny the ladderback
chair actually is. Nevertheless, its
proportions are perfect for the
room in which it sits.

94

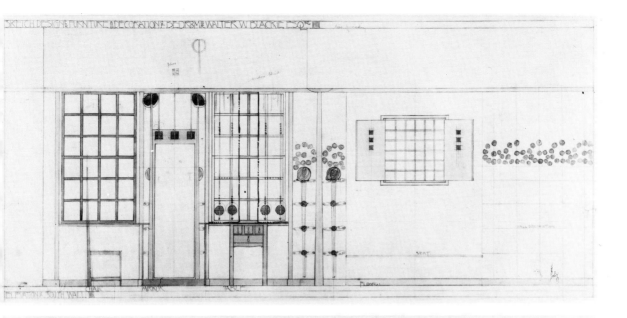

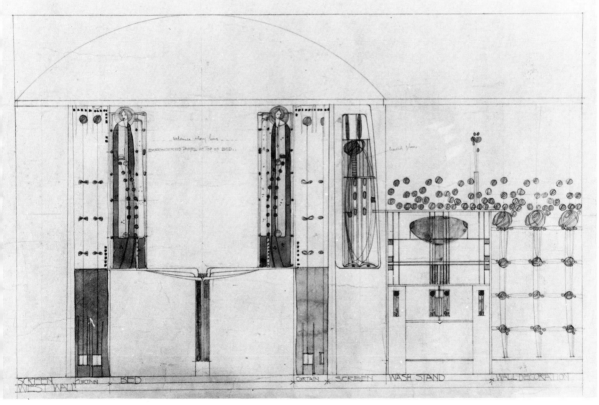

Hill House. Designs for the main bedroom decoration, south and west elevations.

running around the room, familiar from Mackintosh's earlier interiors, from which the main ceiling rises some three feet. The underside of this rail establishes the ceiling levels in the alcoves and determines the height of doors. The higher central 'drum', thus defined, was painted in a very dark sombre colour. The final effect of this treatment is that the main proportion of the room is clearly established, and the resultant panels of doors, walls and alcoves are allowed an easy fluidity.

The main bedroom, again, derives its apparently irregular shape from its pattern of use. The bed is placed in a large alcove off the main

95

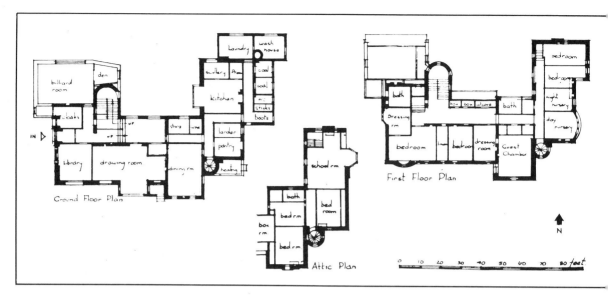

rectangle of the room, on the same pattern as, but on a less lavish scale than, the bedroom in the *Haus eines Kunstfreundes*. Here, too, the same ceiling device is used for defining and linking the spaces, although between the high ceiling level and the lower line of the door, wardrobe and window heads an intermediate element is introduced. The bed alcove has a barrel-vaulted ceiling which springs from the lower level and just touches the higher. This definition of the precise functional allocations within rooms, both in plan and section, followed by the design of fixed and free furniture, gives an extraordinary sensation of organic wholeness; but because of the real grasp and control of the actual functioning of the rooms, they do not have the oppressive immobility often associated with this degree of architectural autonomy. People, curiously enough, are not out of place within them, although it must be acknowledged that certain kinds of furniture would be.

Over the sequence of house designs considered here, a progression, an increasing refinement of intent, can be seen. It is possible, however, to feel that the step from the *Haus eines Kunstfreundes* to Hill House was slightly retrogressive. The latter is more overtly historical in that it is notably more tied to tradition and less completely pictorially resolved in its exterior treatment. But apart from the fact that it is always easier to resolve such a scheme when there is no building budget and no demanding dialogue with a real client, there is every evidence that Mackintosh welcomed the actual exigencies of the real situation as the generators of 'real' architecture, as mentioned in relation to the School of Art scheme. The idea, emanating from the Ruskin and Morris ideologies, of the production of a building as a social process and not a single creative act was with him a firm principle. It was a particularly 'social' process in the case of Hill House, for the Blackie family had an unexpected addition to their family during the course of construction; Mackintosh responded with rare sympathy by creating a nursery at the polar extreme from the master's study.

During the three years (1900–2) in which this series of domestic designs emerged, other events were occurring. The first of these, an event which had the air of the inevitable about it, was his marriage on 22 August 1900 to Margaret Macdonald. There has been, inevitably,

Hill House plans. The dependence on Windyhill, and consequently on Lethaby's The Hurst, is clear. The need to relocate the entrance from the north to the west façade has initiated the most fundamental change, although the larger scale of the house, and the increasing assurance of the architect, have stimulated other detailed developments.

a good deal of idle speculation about the marriage and its effect on the architect's development, and there can be no doubt that Margaret, posthumously, fell prey to the ironies of history. Those critics, starting with P. Morton Shand in his *Architectural Review* articles in 1935, who saw Mackintosh solely as an antecedent of the International Style, and for whom the sole criteria of merit were rectangularity and the absence of ornament, found in Margaret the scapegoat for the decorative predilections in Mackintosh's work they could neither comprehend nor accept. And so, it has been suggested, she impeded him in his unconscious progress towards a twentieth-century ideal.

There is, emphatically, no evidence whatever to support this idea. There is every evidence that he appreciated and encouraged her decorative activities, and that she, in her turn, acknowledged and encouraged his vastly greater gifts. Further, she provided him in a life which became increasingly demanding with much needed support. His personality from the beginning was not marked by stability, and the high bounding enthusiasm and garrulous discussion had their opposites in intense depression and brooding silence. Her constancy and support were unflagging, and their devotion was mutual.

In these early years there was little need of encouragement, with plenty of work at home, and a growing following abroad. The *Dekorative Kunst* article of 1898 had been Mackintosh's introduction to the Continent, and this was followed in the year of his marriage by an invitation to furnish and decorate a room, together with the MacNairs, in the 8th Secessionist Exhibition in Vienna. The bulk of the exhibits were borrowed from work already executed for Glasgow clients. Charles and Margaret went to Vienna, and both they and their work were enthusiastically acclaimed, apparently by critics and public alike, and the triumph was followed by contributions to exhibitions in a number of European centres over the following years. These exhibitions in themselves are not central to the study of Mackintosh's development; they demonstrate Mackintosh's facility in adapting essentially unsuitable space to his own visual requirements, but their constituents were either taken from, or virtually identical to, those he was producing for his clients at home. They brought him into contact with the leaders of change abroad, although, with only one exception, this contact was regrettably on the basis of interior decoration, and not architecture.

That one exception was the *Haus eines Kunstfreundes*, which was published by Koch. This was sufficient to isolate Mackintosh from the other Scottish designers as not only an inventive decorator, but an architect of originality and power. In spite of the masterly quality of the *Haus eines Kunstfreundes* scheme, it is unfortunate that this, rather than his realized buildings, should have been his architectural introduction to Europe. For without an understanding of the designer's background and evolution to this point, it was bound to give a misleading impression. Even Muthesius, who of all Europeans should have understood something of its antecedents, said of the scheme:

The exterior architecture of the building . . . exhibits an absolutely original character, unlike anything else known. In it we shall not find a trace of the conventional forms of architecture, to which the artist, so far as his present intentions were concerned, was quite indifferent.

This was simply not true, although it is easy to see how the design, taken in isolation, could give something of that impression.

Of the various interior design and furnishing commissions executed during these years, it must be noted that all suffered from the initial disadvantage of the exhibition work: that of having to adapt to the strictures of existing buildings. Much could be done, and much was ingeniously done, to alter the visual scale of unsuitable ceiling heights and to mask or alter unsuitable features, but ultimately none of them could have expressed so fully either the architect's intentions of his powers as the interiors of Hill House. It was here, in a building whose every detail was under his direct charge, whose client had real needs and yet every sympathy, that the synthesis of Mackintosh's skills and intentions can first be really felt, and the measure of his genius first appreciated.

Chairs for the Argyle Street Tea Rooms, 1897. Although these chairs predate the commissions from Miss Cranston over which Mackintosh had total control, they anticipate later developments and exhibit some of his difficulties. The immensely tall back rests had the oval panels merely slotted into the uprights. They provided neither stability nor durability. The move from staining to painting or ebonizing his wood followed shortly, for the combination of proportion and adequate joinery details was becoming irreconcilable.

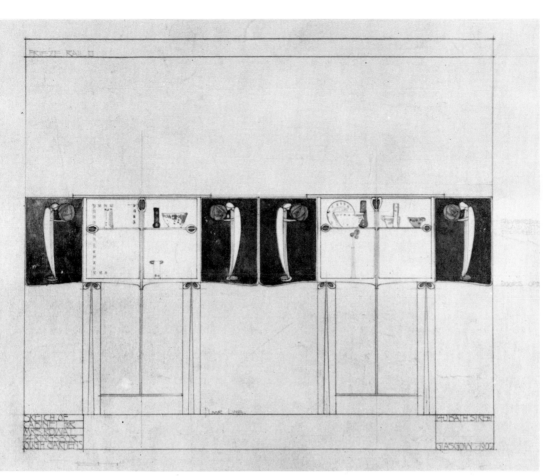

Above Design for two cabinets for
Mrs Rowat, 1902. These cabinets,
which Mackintosh apparently
duplicated with minor alterations
for his own use (*see right*), illustrate
the fluidity which he was
demanding. The furniture is
conceptually no longer wood. It is
simply an appropriately
form-giving material.

CHAPTER SIX:

19°1-4

[The artist] must possess technical invention in order to create for himself suitable processes of expression – and above all he requires the aid of invention in order to transform the elements with which nature supplies him – and compose new images from them.

Writing on the subject of 'Seemliness', Mackintosh tried to sum up his own artistic motivations during these early years of his maturity. And it is this idea of transformation that enabled him to reconcile his acknowledged subservience to Nature with the increasingly abstracted and inventive forms which characterized his work. It was noted that on one occasion he had used the dissected eye of a fish as the theme for decorative exercise, but the principle he was trying to establish here went rather further than the imitation of obscure natural forms.

The artist may have a very rich psychic organisation – an easy grasp and a clear eye for essentials – a great variety of aptitudes – but that which characterises him above all else – and determines his vocation – is the exceptional development of the imaginative faculties – especially the imagination that creates – not only the imagination that represents. The power which the artist possesses of representing objects to himself explains the hallucinating character of his work – the poetry which pervades them – and their tendency towards symbolism – but the creative imagination is far more important. The artist cannot attain to mastery in his art unless he is endowed in the highest degree with the faculty of invention.

He had, of course, established already the principle that this creative effort must not only be stimulated by nature, but must grow out of function:

The only true modern individual art in proportion in form and in colour, is produced by an emotion, produced by a frank and intelligent understanding of the absolute and true requirements of a building or object – a scientific knowledge of the possibilities and beauties of material, a fearless application of emotion and knowledge, a cultured intelligence, and a mind artistic yet not too indolent to attempt the task of clothing in grace and beauty the new forms and conditions that modern development of life – social, commercial, and religious – insist upon.

It is this curious interlocking of intellect and emotion, of function and fantasy, that gives to all his works, but particularly to his interior designs, their fascinating flavour. This is particularly true of the tea room projects for Miss Cranston, over which, after 1901, he had sole professional control. In 1901 he began work on Miss Cranston's premises in Ingram Street, Glasgow. These comprised an extensive

The Willow Tea Rooms, 1902–4. This façade (which has now been virtually restored) shows Mackintosh's deftness in continuing his own increasingly individual manner and yet paying obeisance (albeit cheekily) to his neighbours. There are lessons here about what we now call 'urban infill'.

collection of rooms, to which she added by acquiring leases of adjoining properties. Mackintosh was commissioned to design the interior for the latest of these acquisitions, followed after a lapse of several years by the redesigning of the earlier rooms.

The first of these rooms, the white dining room, is in spirit and detail much like his domestic interiors. But the detail is simpler and more robust, although there is the same attenuated verticality, and the use of thin, flat horizontals as a counter-measure. In terms of 'creative imagination' – as Mackintosh used the words – it is subtly, but not signally different from the domestic interiors of this period.

To see the changes which he could ring with this application of imagination, it is necessary to compare this interior with those for Miss Cranston that followed, in 1902–4 at the Willow Tea Rooms in Sauchiehall Street. But it is important to preface this comparison with the fact that these later rooms cannot be taken to represent a stylistic 'advance'; they were merely imaginatively *different*, for a different set of commercial circumstances. The Willow Tea Rooms were contained in an entirely new building designed by Mackintosh; there were five separate dining or tea rooms, a dining gallery, and a billiards room. The three major dining rooms, or spaces, were open to one another and the furnishings in all were the same. But by his use of the space, the lighting, and the decorative fittings the difference in quality between rooms can be deduced even from pictures. And their collective contrast with the fourth room, the 'Room de Luxe', is even more marked. It can, of course, be argued that these theatricalities were a trivial side issue for a serious architect to undertake, but it cannot be argued so from Mackintosh's own testimony. For these rooms, collectively, demonstrate quite clearly the principles – if so they can be called – that he was attempting to lay down in his lecture. They also demonstrate some other points from that lecture. He referred to the use of 'symbolism' in the arts. The whole of the Willow Tea Rooms were detailed around an elaborate play on the willow-tree form, from which the street name, Sauchiehall, had been derived. Not only was the willow-leaf used as a motif throughout the

Interior of the Willow Tea Rooms showing the wrought-iron balustrades.

decoration, but clearly the abstracted forms of the decorative iron-work, the plaster friezes, and the various fittings were given an imagery relating, however distantly, to tree shapes. The culmination of this 'symbolism' was the gesso panel by Margaret Mackintosh, inspired by Rossetti's sonnet 'O ye, all ye that walk in willow wood', mounted in the 'Room de Luxe'.

Providing the context for this decorative virtuosity was the spatial enclosure of the building itself. Here, for the only time, was Mackintosh able to provide the actual enclosure, and the way in which he shaped and related the spaces is of considerable interest. It was a typical commercial site, facing north on to one of the city's major shopping streets, narrow, deep, and bounded on either side by large, typical buildings.

The building was four storeys high for half the depth from the main street, and a storey and a half, or single storey with gallery, in the rear. This gallery extended from the first landing, about two-thirds of the vertical distance between ground and first floors, and ran around the perimeter of the rear part of the building. A large skylight in the roof of this portion illuminated both the gallery and, through the well, the dining room below. The main stair connecting these spaces was not enclosed, nor was the front edge of the gallery below the ground-floor ceiling. These three major spaces and the stair were thus entirely open to one another and the articulation between them entirely achieved by the disposition of floors and ceilings rather than by walls.

The Willow Tea Rooms Gallery. This photograph of the original interior shows the subtlety of the light both from above and the side.

Much has been made of Mackintosh's play with space as a positive architectural element, and in this building, as much as in any of his work it is easy to see what is meant. But although his manipulation and control were masterly, it would be incautious to use this as a characteristic which set him aside from his contemporaries. It was, after all, a characteristic of both Gothic and Baroque architecture, of Piranesi's prison engravings, of the Crystal Palace, and of any number of Victorian industrial or commercial structures where space was divided for separate, though still public, functions. It was, too, a prime characteristic, and a conscious one, of the all-popular Baillie Scott domestic interiors. And it may fairly be said that Scott display-ed far more conscious interest in 'open planning' than Mackintosh ever did.

None the less, Mackintosh did exploit its possibilities brilliantly. One of the contributory factors to the visual interest was his treat-ment of detail. For his predilection for line and linear ornament tended to give an impression of direction and of surface, but not of mass. Take, for example, his repeated use of simple board-and-batten panelling on walls as in the white dining room at Ingram Street or the sub-gallery dining room at Sauchiehall Street. Whereas con-ventional panelling contains horizontal members with the verticals, thus framing each panel, and the panels themselves are bevelled into the frame, accentuating their proportion and dimension, these are simply linear repeats, slashed by horizontals which are detailed in such a way as to delimit the vertical lines without in any way creating closed forms. This avoidance of closed forms, of static proportions, can be seen too in the vertical stair rods replacing the conventional handrail and balustrading, and in the exposed beam-and-joint sys-tem in the ground-floor ceiling, even to the extent of bringing the joist ends out into the perimeter of the open well, and the beams right through it, as though that well were not a fixed and immutable entity but merely an arbitrary interruption of a linear system.

It is by this treatment, now so familiar in architecture, that the great dynamic illusion of spatial 'interpenetration' is achieved. But it must be noted that the same characteristic applies where there is no intimation of space whatever. For instance, the exteriors of his houses, which are essentially flat surfaces, are given the same kind of flat linear scoring. Here, there is no illusion of 'interpenetration' for there is no attempt to create an ambiguity between solid and void as, for instance, was beginning to appear in Frank Lloyd Wright's houses of the same period. In Mackintosh's houses the voids are unambiguously, albeit erratically, disposed; the solid masses, however, are bent and broken in such a way as to deny any identi-fiable closed geometry. To use an analogy with which he would have been sympathetic, it is an organic rather than a crystalline geometry, the indeterminacy of growing things.

The organic analogy is, of course, one that Mackintosh used himself, and it is easy enough to see how both the approach and the technique were related to his developed graphic techniques and to his neo-Gothic preferences. But there was another underlying reason, one that he hinted at in his lecture on 'Seemliness':

You will never learn to walk so long as there are props. The props of art are –
on the one hand – the slavish imitation of old work – no matter what date or
from what country – and on the other hand the absurd and false idea – that

there can be any living emotion expressed in work scientifically proportioned according to ancient principles – but clothed in the thin fantasy of the author's own fancy.

This prop of ancient proportional principles was becoming at this time a lively issue, and was one of the signs of the growing affection for a disciplined and codified architectural framework for design. It was the general and inevitable reaction of order against chaos, but it was one that Mackintosh, in the certainty and mastery of his own freedom, bitterly opposed. This opposition was even apparent in an area of design where it would appear to be impossible: in the design of furniture.

Of the two basic types of chair seen in the tea rooms – and throughout his work – one was low and more or less cubical, and the

Three characteristic Mackintosh chairs. Although of fundamentally similar construction, their proportional relationships are significantly different.

other was extremely tall. Many of his chairs of the first type were, in fact, based on the cube, that simplest and most static of proportional forms, but the constituent parts were assembled as lapping planes, maintaining their separate identity. The very tall chairs, which tended to be more conventional in their assembly, were none the less so attenuated as to make them entirely linear objects, and to deny any determinate relationship between, say, seat and back. This is easily established by comparing two similar chairs in which the height of the backs differ by several inches, a variation which in conventional chairs would have a critical visual effect, but here becomes quite irrelevant. Similarly in his fondness for thin, overlapping planes as tops for tables, chests of drawers, and indeed buildings, the emphasis is entirely on surface and plane rather than on any precise proportional relationship with the other parts of the assembly.

But Mackintosh's interest in line and surface must not be confused with the latter-day preoccupation with extreme lightness and structural virtuosity. In a paper addressed to a literary society, undated but probably from four to five years after the turn of the century, he discussed architecture under the three traditional heads of strength, usefulness and beauty. In view of the historical position Mackintosh has come to assume, it is worth quoting at length his views on 'strength or stability':

This quality or condition refers to good sound practical workmanship in all the materials, which materials must vary with the locality. Strength itself will be a criterion of the excellency of the architecture, everything approaching the gimcrack or flimsy will condemn the building be it ever so lovely. Of course this does not mean that a summer-house or conservatory be built like a fortress, but it demands that all noble ornament should be of the most enduring material, and placed in the most secure positions. So much in architecture [is] dependent on the quality that it requires not only the real fact but the appearance and will prefer of two equally substantial

Right Slender white painted armchair, with linen-covered drop-in seat which was originally covered in rose silk. The back panel is also linen, printed with a stencilled flower motif. Chairs of this type were produced with minor variations from 1901 or 1902 and variously exhibited in Moscow, Turin and possibly Vienna.

Below Barrel chairs and domino table. The table is almost certainly from the Ingram Street Tea Rooms, possibly 1911, and according to Roger Billcliffe, the chairs were produced some four years earlier. They confirm the diversity of design and feeling in the Mackintosh *oeuvre*.

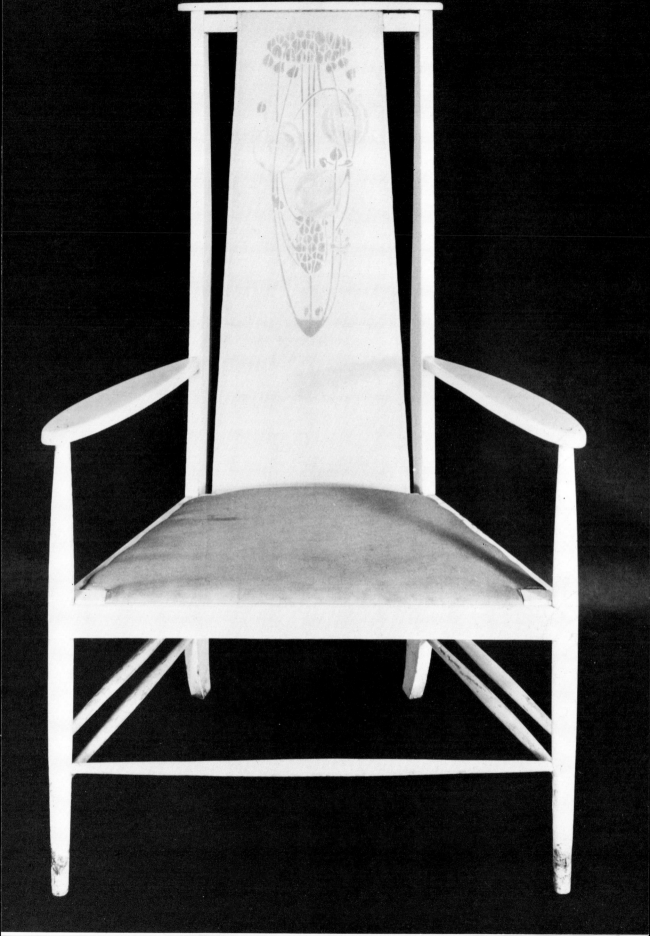

materials the one which has the most bulk. I think that you will admit that it is the want of bulk which is the chief blemish of modern street architecture. Iron is much stronger than stone and so a thin clothes pole of metal is as strong as a much bulkier piece of stone or brick but the eye is distressed at huge lofty tenements resting to all appearance on nothing more stable than plate-glass for the real actual supports are easily overlooked.

These two comparatively modern materials, iron and glass, though eminently suitable for many purposes will never worthily take the place of stone because of this defect – the want of mass. With the advent of the Crystal Palace and the many rose-tinted hallucinations of that period arose the belief in the invention of a new style. At last commonsense, it was shouted, prevails – no more connections with the works of the past – no more deference to the ideas of artists, poets, or even the principles of beauty in nature; for now we can pile up the hugest buildings with the least possible means of support, and that on most economical principles as design can be turned out of the foundry without limit, to the minimising of intellectual labour and so also to the payment of it. But time has passed, and practical experience has shown that apart altogether from any defect in stability or actual comfort the want of appearance of stability is fatal to the introduction of such a style for either domestic, civil, or ecclesiastical buildings. These demand actual mass even if of a weaker material taking bulk for bulk. The leaning tower of Pisa though abundantly strong as has been proved by centuries, is yet tottering and insecure to all appearance, some say so much as that to sleep under its tottering shadow would be almost impossible. Thus in this quality of architecture mind and body must be considered. Egyptian remains will always impress the mind in a way Chinese flippery never will. The Alhambra, gorgeous and refined in its ornament though it was, more beautiful than perhaps any other building, yet because its materials are but plaster, wood, porcelain and tile work, is yet of a lower type of architecture than the far plainer but more enduring country churches of England or Normandy.

It would be well, then, to pass on that note from the Willow Tea Rooms – Mackintosh's 'Alhambra' – to his 1903 submission for the Liverpool Cathedral competition. It is, whatever else, massive. It is also in its plan, disposition, structure and materials, entirely traditional. Within this traditional framework, the forms and details are firmly within, and directly derived from, the modern Gothic idiom, although in their outworking they would doubtless be stamped with the characteristic Mackintosh flavour. There is no evidence here – nor is there any in his writing – to suggest any ideological change from the time of the Queen's Cross project, or even, perhaps, the Soane Medallion design of the railway terminus, although there is much more competence and a clearer purpose. And, by comparison, the scheme is less adventurous than the submission of Lethaby and E. S. Prior, and even less so than Bentley's Westminster Cathedral in London, then nearing completion.

So the picture of Mackintosh as a conscious pioneer of modernity must be carefully qualified. He was certainly firmly committed to the principle of producing an architecture of his own time; he was quite prepared to break with precedent to serve a new function or explore a new imagery; he was violently opposed to any suggestion of historical mummery. But he was equally committed to preserving a visible and meaningful continuity with the past, to using old materials in the old ways, and to respecting old conventions for old functions.

In the foregoing paper, Mackintosh discussed at some length the problem of beauty in architecture, and it reveals a good deal about not only his attitudes but the buildings themselves. He began by

Liverpool Cathedral competition, 1903. Perspective and plan. The power of this proposal has too often been overlooked by later commentators in their search for 'modernity'. There is also an unconfirmed hint in the Mackintosh legend that Charles Reilly, the influential Professor at the Liverpool School of Architecture, may have had a hand in its rejection. If that had been the case, it would almost certainly have been because it was deemed too modern.

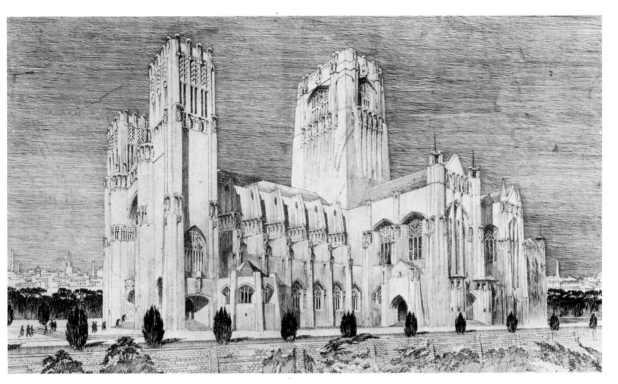

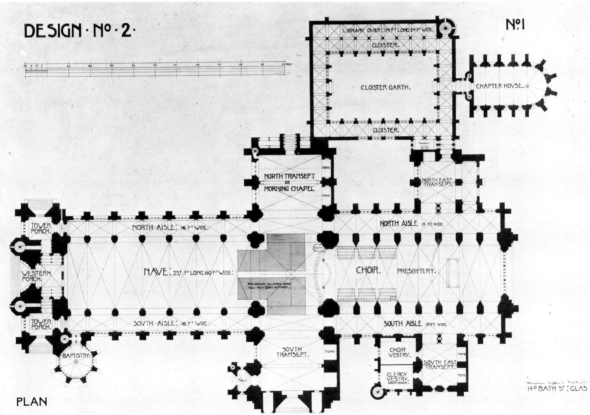

foundering nobly on the rock of 'Taste'. This effort though admittedly unsuccessful was not without significance, for there were two contemporary ways of dealing with the problem, either one of which would have navigated him past it. One was the attitude of the Lethaby group, from William Morris, which saw in the very concept

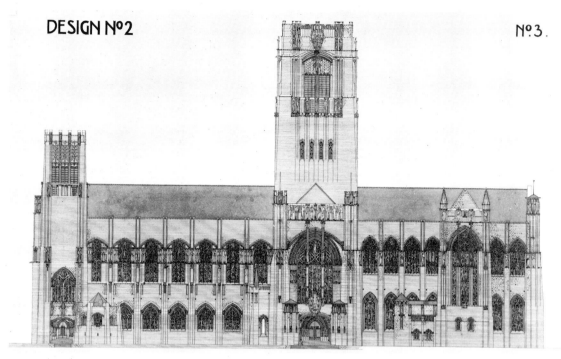

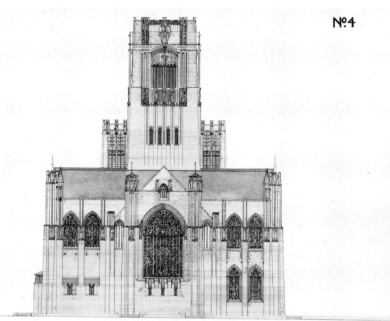

Liverpool Cathedral competition. South and east elevations. If these are compared with his student Railway Terminus scheme, one can see how much of the 'traditional' language of architecture remained entirely valid for Mackintosh, and yet to what more powerful purpose he was able to use it now.

of Taste the distillation of all that was wrong with contemporary attitudes towards culture. They maintained simply that it did not or should not exist beyond entirely rational appropriateness; that any idea of a special 'gift' or cultivated sensibility beyond the thorough and workmanlike exploration of defined problems was a snare and a snobbish delusion. The other school seemed in many respects virtually to confirm the objections of the first. For they, admitting with Ruskin this special sensibility, and yet despairing of its definition, fell back on history. They saw in, or read into, the past and most readily the past of the Renaissance, convenient canons which could be learned and taught, and which could provide cultural anchors in the world of volcanic change which surrounded them.

Mackintosh rejected both. And it was this rejection which, as much as any other factor, isolated him from the support and approbation of his British contemporaries. He deplored the reversion to outmoded rules, yet he would allow of neither anarchy in matters of taste, nor of its unconscious assimilation:

The faculty of distinguishing good from bad in design is a faculty which most educated people – and especially ladies – conceive they possess. How it has been acquired few would be able to explain. The general impression seems to be that it is the peculiar inheritance of gentle blood, and independent of all training that while a young lady is devoting at school, or under a governess, so many hours a day to music, so many to languages, and so many to general science, she is all the time unconsciously forming that sense of the beautiful which we call taste, that the sense once developed will enable her unassisted by any special study or experience not only to appreciate the charms of nature in every aspect, but to form a correct estimate of the merits of works in architecture, painting, sculpture, etc. That this impression had gained ground may be inferred from the fact that there is no single point on which well-educated women are more jealous of disparagement than in this. We may condemn a lady's opinion in politics – criticise her handwriting – correct her pronunciation of Latin and disparage her favourite authors with a chance of escaping displeasure, but if we venture to question her taste in the most trivial matter we are sure to offend.

The argument is good, but the spirit is better; this man had built houses. Yet he was insistent that this 'sense of the beautiful' had a real and objective existence. This reality was to be discovered through certain 'principles of beauty which are common to . . . all true beauty'.

The first of these was 'Truth'. And truth in architecture,

. . . is only present when every material is shown on its own merits and mimics not the resemblance of any others. Thus it may be necessary in a brick wall to weather-proof it – internally or externally it does not matter – with plaster or cement which may be done and no deceit shown but the practice is detestable where it is scored over to delude into the belief that stone is used.

He then went on to discuss the use of other veneering and finishing materials – gilding and marble veneering were acceptable because of the well-understood costliness of the materials, and thus no sham was implicit; paint was to be used on woodwork in preference to graining, and an even better solution was the use of coloured stains revealing the actual grain of the material. Cast-iron 'can be a useful and at the same time beautiful object, but it is not improved when with imitation rivet heads it tries to pass for hand-wrought metal work or by paint for bronze'.

But matters such as these were 'but the auxiliaries of architecture'. The same principle when applied to the fundamentals of architectural design forbade such frauds as he had deplored on his youthful visit to Siena, and such devices as the erection of tall gables before low-pitched roofs,

. . . gables that are simply masks, not the decoration and expressions of the necessities of the buildings, but to meet the supposed requirements of the Gothic style they are lofty and steeply pitched, so that only a view from another point of view than that intended by the architect discloses the sham.

Wren's St Paul's duly received its traditional moral censure for its 'false' upper storey, and he then went on to define another principle of 'Beauty':

That construction should be decorated, and not decoration constructed. . . . thus the salient and most requisite features should be selected for ornamentation, so from this it must appear that, windows and doors being about the most important of modern requirements, round these should any ornament be sought. Yet note how this is forgotten in a type of building you are all acquainted with – the classic churches in vogue 20 years ago . . . which you will note depend for architectural effect on the application of flat columns attached to the walls in imitation of the temple style, while the windows and doors are simply holes in the walls – observe I am not complaining of plainness when little money can be got but of misapplication of money when obtained.

And so he went on with the kind of Puginesque argument that had been familiar for half a century or more.

His next principle was one which, in view of his work, may be somewhat surprising:

Yet one other powerful element in Beauty is association or tradition, which will modify the force of laws which in the abstract are admitted to be correct and true and grant a certain . . . [sic] to local or national customs or to practices sanctioned of high authority. When Burns in his *Cotter's Saturday Night* after enumerating some of our favourite psalm tunes burst out 'compared wae they Italian trills are tame', as a piece of musical criticism it may not hold true world-wide yet it is a very sufficient reason and obvious truth to Scotsmen, so in the same manner there are many decorative features in Scotch architecture, which might well be replaced by others of antiquity yet just because we are Scotch and not Greek or Roman we reject. For example there is the quaint old Scotch gate pillars with the spire resting on 3 or 4 stone bullets – the curious balls often seen at stairs . . . and very many other features which give a historical character to the building they adorn. . . . In fact I think we should be a little less cosmopolitan and rather more national in our architecture, as we are with language, new words and phrases will be incorporated gradually, but the wholesale introduction of Japanese sentiment for example would be denounced and rightly by the purist.

But then, having admitted the role of the traditional, he had to give an immediate corrective:

Still of course this conservatism is often made a cloak for and excuse for mediocrity in design and the causeless and unceasing repetition of features which have only their age to recommend them; and so Variety and Novelty if not carried too far, are qualities both allowable and desirable, but by ignorance often clamoured for most unreasonably.

The inadequacy of his argument is a fair reflection of the quandary of the times. But the very points he raised as principles of beauty were those that had motivated the whole post-Pugin phase of the Gothic Revival, and through the whole of this argument, as through all of his writing, his affection for the Gothic is clear. At one point in his lecture he even mentioned with favour Sir Gilbert Scott's treatment of St Mary's Cathedral in Edinburgh. This, of course, did not make him a Gothic Revivalist; but the firm allegiance to these principles, the self-evident way in which they influenced his work, and his confessed admiration for the leading figures in that succession, place him clearly and precisely in the British picture.

Why then was he not recognized and acclaimed within it? There are a number of contributory answers, but their force was not to be appreciated until after 1910 when his full development was realized in the completion of the School of Art, and when, tragically, his effective architectural output was finished.

CHAPTER SEVEN:
1904-9

In 1904 John Honeyman retired and Mackintosh became an official partner in the firm, thenceforth known as Honeyman, Keppie and Mackintosh. It seems clear that relations within the firm were amicable enough, although there is no evidence to suggest any degree of intimacy between Mackintosh and either of his senior partners, in spite of the fact that Keppie was only six years older. Nor is there any evidence in the work of the firm that Mackintosh's personal style had any marked effect on other projects. Since the time of the competition for the Glasgow School of Art, however, it is clear that he had considerable or complete autonomy in the projects assigned to him. Indeed, in view of his considerable independent success, it is unthinkable that he would have remained in the firm had this not been the case.

After the Liverpool Cathedral competition scheme, Mackintosh began work on a new Glasgow school. Scottish primary and secondary education was generally acknowledged, with that of Germany, to have the most advanced national level in Europe, and a fundamental policy of Scottish education, unlike that of England, was that it should be coeducational. The school that Mackintosh designed represented the usual Scottish pattern, comprising a collection of classrooms, a large assembly and drill hall, and a cookery

Scotland Street School, 1903–07. Perspective.

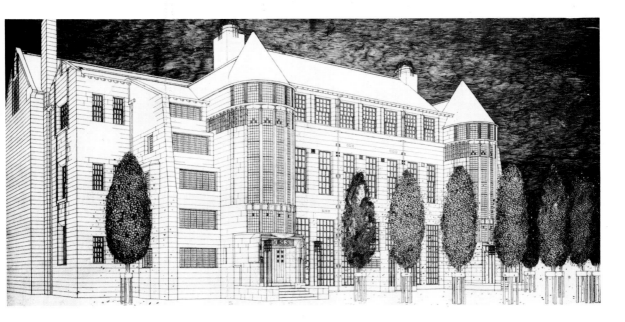

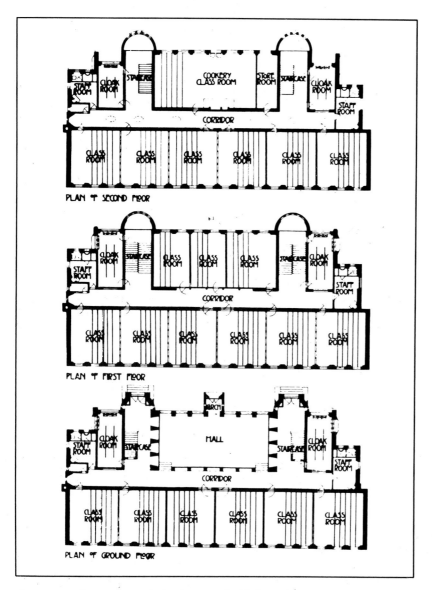

PLAN OF SECOND FLOOR

PLAN OF FIRST FLOOR

PLAN OF GROUND FLOOR

Left Scotland Street School Plan, and *Right* the entrance elevation. The clarity, economy, and apparent functionalism of this building have made it a favourite with those who claim Mackintosh as a pioneer of the Modern Movement. Yet the antecedents of all its elements are clear in his earlier work, and it was designed almost at the same time as his scheme for Liverpool Cathedral.

classroom; lavatory and cloakroom facilities ranked beside the separate stair towers for each sex. The simple, direct bifurcation of the plan is the direct acknowledgement of this most symmetrical of programmes.

The stringent cost controls exercised then, as now, on school building is reflected not only by the economy of the plan but in the elimination of extraneous detail inside and outside the finished building. Such decorative detail as there is has been concentrated, in accordance with his expressed theory, around doors and windows. And while the forms, by hindsight can be taken, and have been taken, as extremely prophetic of the new architecture, they belong, in their essence, equally with the building forms of their own time. Perhaps not surprisingly, in trying to exploit what Mackintosh called 'the spirit of the old' without slavishly emulating its details, he produced a building with the 'spirit of the new'. Indeed, it could fairly be said that the construction of the walls, the framing around window openings, the forms of the roofs and the building materials are all in accord with those of the tenement buildings which had become, notoriously, the main building fabric of the city during the

Left Scotland Street School.
Interior of the entrance bay.

Below The Music Room,
Hous'hill, 1904. The curve of the
screen is picked up and reinforced
by recurrent circles throughout the
room.

nineteenth century. What transform their use in this instance are the clear and orderly disposition of the plan elements expressed in the building form, the size and proportions of the windows in response to the functional needs, and the precise visual relationships established by this master graphic artist.

It is worth speculating on the different image Mackintosh might have presented to the world had his two major monuments, aside from domestic building, not been educational establishments severely strictured by cost. It is certain that his reputation would not have been less, and probably would have been in his own time considerably greater, but it would also have been somewhat different. For the decorative restraint that characterizes these buildings, and which made such critics as Gleeson White hail him as a prophet of machine-age architecture, was to Mackintosh a question of what Pugin called 'propriety'. Scotland Street School represented one end of a social hierarchy whose other end, and whose pinnacle, was represented by Liverpool Cathedral, and the rich iconography and decorative embellishment of the one was as valid a social response as the restraint of the other.

During the period from initial design to the completion of construction of the Scotland Street School, that is from 1903 to 1906, Mackintosh was engaged in the construction of the Willow Street Tea Rooms, and in the conversion and interior design of a large house for Miss Cranston and her husband, Major Cochrane.

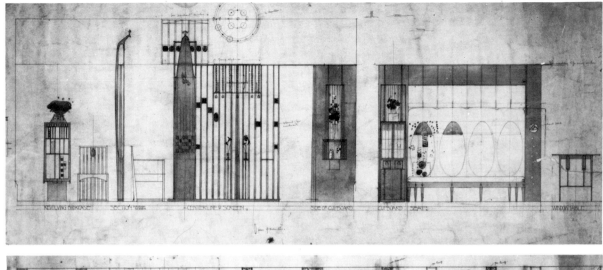

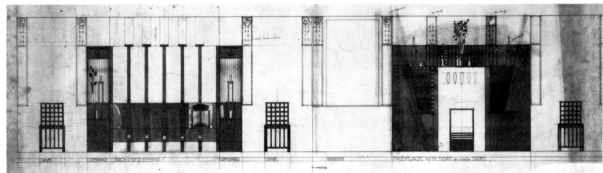

Top Elevation of the Music Room, Hous'hill.
Bottom Elevation of the Blue Bedroom, Hous'hill.

In the decorations for this house, there are no appreciable differences in principle from the domestic interiors of the previous years, or from the tea room designs. The work consisted primarily of refurbishing and refurnishing existing interiors, and while many of the bits he designed had the expected ingenuity and originality, in only one instance was he able to manipulate the interior space itself. This was in the music room, whose one end, as existing, was semi-circular in plan. He exploited this by poising a flat horizontal member – rather like his usual picture rail – in a continuous circle concentric with, and some two feet within, the end wall. This member was supported on the room side by a screen of vertical slats for a segment of its length, and on the curved-wall side by typical built-in fittings, benches and window seats. It is a characteristic instance of his demarcation of functional areas within a single space, and if a little more overt than in the earlier domestic interiors, may well have been due to his experience with larger scale spatial relationships at the Willow Tea Rooms.

There exist two brief accounts of meetings with Mackintosh during this period, when he was in his middle thirties, and at the height of his success. The first, by E. B. Kalas, was published in *De la Tamise à la Sprée: L'essor des industries d'art* in 1905. Kalas went, as on a pilgrimage, to meet the Mackintoshes in their flat in 120 Mains Street, Glasgow. His style is florid, and his tone eulogizing, but the description is of interest:

Meet . . . the occupants of this house of white and violet. A gentleman, thirty-five years old, tall, dressed all in black, with long dark hair parted in the middle; the eyes slumber in their setting of bushy eyebrows but flame up

118

from their gloom in occasional flashes of vari-coloured sparks; the mouth betrays caution, perhaps timidity – probably mockery. The general appearance is of a clean-shaven American clergyman who is still pulsing with the emotion and travail of his last metaphysical discourse but has succeeded, by powers of restraint, in preserving an impassivity and an unnatural silence – Charles Rennie Mackintosh.

He was probably not far off the mark. The other, by Desmond Chapman-Huston, was written in retrospect from 1949, and marked the first meeting of what was to become a lifelong friendship. The one personal observation that Chapman-Huston made was that he immediately and instinctively felt himself to be in the presence of a great man; whether the impression was the creation of memory cannot be known. But it does seem clear that this strong vein of brooding intensity was even then sufficiently marked to set him apart in the minds of those who met him. Chapman-Huston recalled also a reference by Charles to his wife's work: 'Margaret has genius; I have only talent.' The myopia of love is a common enough phenomenon, nevertheless the sentiment bespeaks more than a reluctant toleration of her decorative enterprises.

In establishing an accurate chronology of design for such an architect as Mackintosh, it is important to realize the sometimes considerable duration of time required for building and the consequent overlap of one scheme with another. This constructional overlap is of some importance, for to a man of his design philosophy, the designing process never stopped until the builder had literally left the premises. Thus, for example, Hill House was not actually completed until the spring of 1904, by which time the Willow Tea Rooms were under way, the Liverpool Cathedral scheme was over a year behind, and the Scotland Street School design work had begun. Concurrently, a number of decorative commissions had been and were being carried out. It was a period of intense – in view of the attention he lavished on his work, phenomenally intense – production, and the climax by which history knows him began in the following year, 1905, with the design revisions for the completion of the School of Art.

The startling changes that emerged in the completion of this building in 1909 reveal both the changes that had taken place in Mackintosh's personal manner over the decade since the first design, and those principles which were the underlying, and unchanging, constants in his work.

The only parts of the west wing which remained substantially unchanged from the initial scheme were the major north-facing studios and their elevation to the street. For the rest, some changes were the result of functional requirements, and some merely the detailed outworking of his mature style and his accumulated experience.

One of the weaknesses in the original scheme which, at this stage, had to be corrected, was the inadequacy of escape stairs in case of fire. He accordingly introduced two new stairs in the re-entrant angles at each end of the south face, one of which had of course to be connected to the existing structure. This easternmost stair passed by and obstructed two of the existing windows to the original boardroom on the first floor. In his quixotic treatment of this problem can be seen his attachment to the Arts and Crafts principle of building design as a social document – that it should tell in its fabric not only of the needs that brought it into being, but of the changing circumstances of its history and adaptation. Rather than remove the windows, which could no longer serve the room with light, and which in any event were shallow protruding bays which obstructed the clear run of the stair, he carefully left them in place, with obscured glass, and tortuously formed the run of treads around them.

The south elevation, abutting and overhanging a miscellaneous collection of buildings – then and now – is an agglomeration of such responses to the calls of Nature: there are minor elements which preserve a tenuous, though half-hearted, acknowledgement of symmetry, but they are overwhelmed by the enthusiastic accretions called into being by change. An extra storey was incorporated in this second stage, providing masters' studios; it created a problem of access to alternate staircases, since the existing Director's studio effectively barred passage from one end to the other. Mackintosh solved the problem by building the upper two storeys of the new wing to the full depth of the floors below, and then spanning the gap behind the Director's studio with a cantilevered gallery, known as

Left Glasgow School of Art. The east staircase, passing the window of the original Board Room. Note how the treads are shortened to accommodate the bay in the most casual manner.
Right The east staircase at first floor level.

the 'hen-run' and looking for all the world like a segment of tram-car tacked on to the face of the building. So it went, inventing, adapting, creating, with a compulsive restlessness that makes the whole assembly a warren of discovery.

What this process cost the clients in patience and money can only be guessed at, but it was probably only the support of Newbery that made the adventure possible. What it cost the builders in exasperation and ingenuity will never be known either, but there were two occasions when tradesmen downed tools at the demands the architect was making of them. One of these was in connection with the plastering of ogival-shaped corridor-ceiling light wells, and the other, the execution of complex linear 'knots' in the ends of wrought-iron 'tee' beams which protruded into one of the minor studios. Since each of these 'knots' was different, and they occurred roughly every six feet for the length of the studio, the objections can be understood, and it is a tribute of a sort that the architect not only succeeded in persuading the workmen to return in both cases, but to carry out the details as intended.

In connection with this unremitting inventiveness, however, there are two characteristics that stand out unusually forcibly. First, no matter how outrageous the distortion, the decorative details always spring from some functional or constructional demand – they are 'decorated construction'. Second, for all the spaces in the building

Glasgow School of Art. *Above* The 'loggia' and 'hen-run'.
Below Wrought-iron 'knots' in cantilevered 'tee' beams. *Right* Exterior view of the 'hen-run'.

which are not set aside for 'prestige' reasons – such as the boardroom – the materials he exposed and played with are almost perversely crude. He used rough sawn timber, exposed, plated and rivetted steel and iron structural members, rough brickwork, and trowelled but unfinished cement rendering. The fact that the elimination of some of the wilder details might well have paid for more ordinary and perhaps pretentious finishes is irrelevant. He was dramatically exploiting a state of ruthless economy, even if in a somewhat uneconomical manner, and the resulting interiors have a rugged workmanlike quality entirely in keeping with their function seventy years since.

Left Glasgow School of Art. Interior of one of the studios. The easels are believed to have been designed by Mackintosh.
Right Studio above the library. The tall columns are in fact steel, although the very Japanese beam and bracket arrangement at the top would suggest otherwise. The columns are on the line of those in the library below.

But one of the interior spaces where wet canvases and plaster droppings would not intrude was the library, and it is here that the case for Mackintosh the pioneer of modernism finally focuses. The room is basically as indicated on the 1896 drawings, a thirty-five foot square some seventeen feet high, or two-thirds of the height of the studios. An open gallery encircles the upper part of the room, creating within the square of the room a slightly oblong open well. But whereas the gallery on the original drawings was conventionally supported from below, the supporting structure and all the detailed handling that springs from it are, in the finished product, entirely different.

The finished gallery is supported by two rows of columns running east and west, and extending upwards to provide support for the ceiling above. The rows of columns are equally spaced across the room, that is between eleven and twelve feet apart, but the galleries are only some eight feet deep – the space required for their function. As a result, the gallery beams are extended outward in pairs to grip the columns, as it were, in space. It is a structural play that has raised inevitable, and often excited, comment. But, not immediately obvious, there is a sound structural reason for the arrangement, and it springs from the fact that the library is but one apartment in a structure of several storeys.

Below and *Right* Glasgow School of Art. The library.

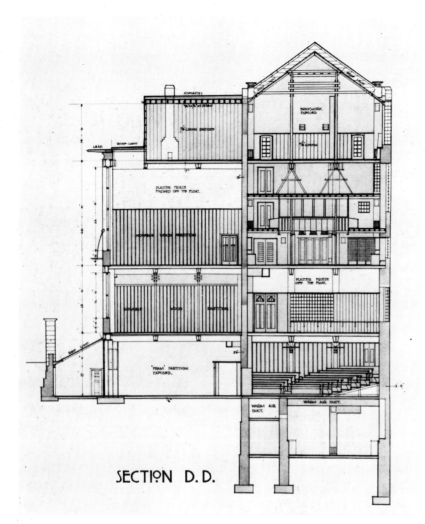

SECTION D.D.

Glasgow School of Art.
Left Section through the west
wing, showing the relationship
between the library and the rooms
above and below.

In the cross-section through the library wing the construction of
the two floors immediately below the library can be seen as consisting
of pairs of steel beams spanning east to west, creating three equal
spans for the wood joist floors. The lines of these beams were, in fact,
the only reasonable points from which the library gallery could be
supported, and the positions from which structural continuity could
be established with the floors above. This simple reason for the basic
structural system detracts in no way from the visual drama which
Mackintosh has then built around his solution, but it does justify,
according to his own principles, a detail which might otherwise be
seen as a purely arbitrary tour-de-force. It is interesting in this regard
to compare this interior with one almost exactly contemporary, the
design for the Oak Room, in Miss Cranston's Ingram Street Tea
Rooms. While the similarity in the detailing is quite obvious, the Oak
Room, being merely the refurbishing of an existing interior, with
neither the structural problem nor the opportunities of the library,
has in turn none of its spatial interest.

It would seem that in the structuring of a space out of timber, all
Mackintosh's various skills and preoccupations could happily run
together – the interest in problems of structural assembly, his
experience as a designer of furniture, his fascination with line and
surface, and his happy fusion of tradition and inventiveness. The
traditions he acknowledges in the library interior are clear, but the

Right First floor Museum,
showing the stair-well rising into
the centre of the space, and the
very definite Japanese influence of
the roof construction.

Left Glasgow School of Art. Library from gallery level.

acknowledgement is anything but servile. To use his own words, he would not be guilty of 'feebly imitating some of the visible and superficial features of beautiful old works and neglecting the spirit, the intention, the soul that lies beneath'. Certainly the spirit of many kinds of old works can be seen, although the forms are never quite the same. The whole approach to the beam-and-column framing is reminiscent of the Japanese, and at the same time perhaps of Gothic architecture, in the way the columns pick up the loading of the gallery beams by means of extra members, 'cluster piers', clamped on the sides of the main columns. And there are odd Arts and Crafts whimsicalities, such as patterns of tiny protruding dowels at tenoned joints, and the graphic use of the old English device called the 'waggon chamfer' on the free balusters seen between the columns and the solid gallery balustrade. The waggon chamfer is the pattern of small successive bites taken out of the edges of rectangular wooden members, and belonged traditionally to the coach-building and waggon-building crafts. It was introduced as a decorative device for furniture and architecture by the short-lived Kenton & Co., whose moving spirits were Lethaby, Reginald Blomfield, Sydney and Ernest Barnsley, and Ernest Gimson. The device, and variations on it, became subsequently almost a hallmark of the Cotswold work of Gimson and the brothers Barnsley, and it is probably no coincidence to see it emerging in Mackintosh's vocabulary.

But in spite of the presence of such elements, the all-too-quaint nostalgia of the Arts and Crafts mentality, which had been evident in his handling of the timber framing of the School's main stair and museum, had now quite disappeared. There is a crispness, an incisiveness, which we recognize as being wholly modern in feeling, even though it is emphatically not revolutionary in intent.

Right Glasgow School of Art. Bay windows in the library showing the recessed gallery balustrade and the recessed wall of the law room introduced between the library and the top studio.

It is on the west façade, generated by and expressive of this library interior, that the modern feeling reaches perhaps its highest pitch. Yet here again it is a question of feeling, of the architect's individual handling of the forms, rather than of the origin of the forms themselves or their material. Characteristically, the disposition of the windows and their sizes is a direct reflection of the plan. And their grouping into continuous vertical bays is a grammatical device initiated by Norman Shaw, picked up by Voysey, Lethaby and any number of late Victorians – and, of course, used by Mackintosh himself ten years before at the main entrance to this self-same building, with the linking of the ground-floor office and the Director's room. This particular relationship is rather important to an understanding of much of Mackintosh's formal handling, for he undoubtedly used such devices as these as 'motifs', in a compositional approach analogous to music. In his lecture on 'Seemliness' he had said:

What one misses in . . . most . . . is – the large rhythm that undulates through that of the great masters ancient and modern – the sustained note of informing purpose – the deep vibration of some unifying undertone now rising to accent and emphasis – now sounding faintly, beneath the multifariousness of accompanying motives – but always visible to an attentive sense as the basis if not the burden of the theme with variations – the ensemble which every artist's work – no matter how trivial, should constitute.

Taken in this way, it can be seen how the form of the bay window at the main entrance, and its faint echo in the engaged octagonal tower on the east face, was picked up as a linking theme and a point of departure for the treatment of the new wing. It is the dominant form on the west façade, and then around the corner on the south it is repeated, this time inset flush with the face of the wall. It then recurs, squatter and fatter, as three seating alcoves on the south face of the top-floor loggia.

Glasgow School of Art. *Left* Light pendant and decorated pilasters in the new Board Room.
Right Window seats in the west corridor leading to the Library.

Central Reference Library, Bristol, by H. Percy Adams, 1893. The building was designed by Charles Holden and the design was published in *The Builder* in 1895.

But having acknowledged the provenance of the bays, it is still startlingly apparent that there is a great change in the manner of their use, the difference that is apparent between the handling of the east and west elevations of the building. This is, of course, a measure of Mackintosh's development over the intervening decade, a similar contrast as between the Martyr's Public School and the Scotland Street School. But it is also a measure of the change in British architecture generally, and the west façade can be related as directly to some contemporary building as could the east. Summerson has pointed out the similarity in treatment between the west wing and Charles Holden's design for the Central Reference Library in Bristol, drawings of which were published in *The Builder* for 2 September 1895, and which would almost certainly be known to Mackintosh. There is also, for what it is worth, a remote kind of ideological link-up between the work of the two men. Mackintosh was confessedly an admirer of J. D. Sedding, and elements of Sedding and of his pupil Henry Wilson are apparent in much of Mackintosh's work, particularly in the ecclesiastical designs. Holden in his turn admitted to being at this period chiefly indebted in his work to Henry Wilson. In other of Holden's designs of this period, too, there can be seen the same rigid, attenuated rectangularity although without perhaps the drama of Mackintosh's work, notably the British Medical Association building in the Strand, London, and in the extension to the Law Society headquarters in Chancery Lane.

The British Medical Association headquarters in the Strand, London, by Charles Holden, 1906–07.

Summerson has also drawn attention to the 'acute experience – direct or indirect – of Michelangelo' in Mackintosh's library wing, and evident in much of the English work of the period. There is reason to believe that this very evident interest in and sympathy with the drama and distortion of Michelangelo's architecture was related to the general interest in the 'transitional' styles of architecture referred to earlier. Many architects, including Mackintosh, were much more interested in the possibility of manipulation and synthesis of historical elements than in the analysis and faithful reproduction of entire historical vocabularies. And certainly the interest in Michelangelo was marked at this time. Beresford Pite, with whose work Mackintosh was familiar – notably the Institute of Chartered Accountants building produced under John Belcher's name – wrote a long and detailed study on Michelangelo's architecture in the *Architectural Review* during 1900, and Pite's successor as Belcher's 'ghost', John James Joass, produced in London the Royal Insurance Company building in 1907 with as clear an indebtedness to Michelangelo as any English building has had.

Joass had been trained in Glasgow under John Burnet, and was probably a personal acquaintance of Mackintosh. At any rate, there is a notable kinship which might have been more evident had the prepared cylinders in Mackintosh's library windows ever received their intended figure sculpture.

There is a pencilled note on Mackintosh's contract drawings which seems to indicate his intention that three of these figure carvings were to be of Cellini, St Francis and Palladio. An ill-assorted trio, and yet curiously apposite, for Mackintosh's central architectural achievement may well be regarded as the dramatic reconciliation of strange bedfellows. This certainly is what the completed School represents; it is an incredible and effective fusion of a whole series of different and disparate streams evident on the British scene in the last decade of the nineteenth century and the first of this. There is no element in the building which cannot be related, directly or indirectly, to contemporary British work, and the fact that many of the sources for his inspiration regarded themselves as mutually exclusive can be forgotten in the entity of this building.

Yet there is no evidence that Mackintosh was trying – in twentieth-century terms – to be modern. He was certainly not trying to create a new technological image; exposed steel, plate glass and concrete were not considered remarkable enough for special comment at the time, being simply the expression of the particular economy of the building, and the entire emphasis is on those hand-wrought elements made from traditional materials. Nor was he overtly expressing a new attitude to space – although his handling of space was superb – for in the only part of this building where the spatial emphasis is unusual, it grew from a particular structural context. Nor was he preoccupied with structural virtuosity for its own sake, although he exploited structure as a springboard for decorative fancy. For some curious reason, the small flower-conservatory projecting from the upper south face of the library wing has suggested to some a great structural daring. But this is not the clear cantilever it appears to be from some points of view, lying as it does in the re-entrant angle between the studio wall and the stair wall; it has a respectable ancestry in a hundred Scottish and French castle walls, and it lies, after all, only a cannon shot from the Clyde, beside whose everyday engineering practice it paled, even then, into insignificance.

Nevertheless, the School of Art represents an earnest attempt to be 'modern' – not in twentieth-century terms, but in nineteenth. Its emphasis was not on technology, space and structure, but on function, method and iconography.

CHAPTER EIGHT:

19°9-28

The School of Art was completed in 1909. During the three years involved in the design and construction of the second phase, Mackintosh had designed several tea rooms for Miss Cranston, continued work on her residence Hous' hill, and designed at least two other houses, Mosside in Kilmacolm, and Auchenibert in Killearn, in neither of which had he been blessed with the degree of client support provided in the earlier house projects, and in neither of which had the vision and promise of the earlier houses been retained.

From work done recently by Dr Frank Walker, the work at Mosside, or Cloak as it is now more correctly known, was a series of design and extension works carried out for H. B. Collins, a mining engineer. The work appears to have extended between 1906 and 1913. Indeed, the final work by Mackintosh on this building may well have been his last architectural contribution in Scotland.

The series of studies and extensions of that house are instructive – not for the monumental importance of the resulting building, but almost for the opposite. It requires a very discerning eye indeed to see the hand of the great architect at work. It is principally an exercise in a very ordinary Scottish vernacular, not dissimilar to the humbler productions of, say, Robert Lorimer.

Added to this, his manner of working was not designed to endear him to either his clients or his partner. In the pursuit of perfection, the changes, the voluminous detailing, the demands on time and skill from building operatives, took account of neither his clients' nor his own firm's purse or patience. Others who had used this particular approach to building design had experienced similar difficulty. Philip Webb, the archetype, had never undertaken more than a single job at a time, and his income throughout a notable and immensely influential career had never been more than barely sufficient for his own modest needs. Lethaby, again highly respected and influential, effectively retired from active building from 1904, at the age of forty-seven, due to the nervous strain imposed by it. And Mackintosh, whose collective output during these years was considerable, and whose authoritarian approach did not ease the demands, must have suffered stresses that can only be guessed at. A joiner who had worked under his direction on furniture commissions recalled wryly after half a century: 'There was nae palaver wi' Charlie.' He would brook no opposition in the pursuit of his objectives.

In all this he had, of course, the unabated support of his Continental admirers. But, flattering as it must have been, it was not the support he most needed. What he needed above all was the support of those at home who could both provide more amenable working opportunities, and who could understand and share a common architectural heritage. There is no evidence that his Continental emulators appreciated anything in his architectural work beyond its graphic and decorative mannerism and the more self-evident aspects of its functionalism.

Thus as Mackintosh reached an effective architectural maturity, he almost concurrently found himself in an isolation which was becoming unbearable. And over the four years from the completion of the School of Art in 1909 to 1913, his architectural output was marginal.

During 1910 and 1911 Mackintosh was engaged on the last two interiors at Miss Cranston's Ingram Street Tea Rooms, the Cloister Room and the Chinese Tea Room. These are of interest in that they show more markedly a stylistic development that was emerging in his last work at the School of Art. This was the preoccupation with severely rectilinear forms, not just for the constructive framework for his buildings and furniture, but for the decorative patterns as well. The long, complex curves of his early graphic manner were virtually gone, and were being replaced by a much more staccatto ornamentation rather like the waggon-chamfering in the library interior, and the parallel zig-zags seen on the architrave of the west entrance. These two motifs, indeed, form almost the entire basis for the decoration of the Cloister Room, and they produce a character markedly different from any of the earlier interiors and certainly not as clearly resolved. The China Tea Room is also strongly rectilinear, this time composed of repetitive squares in the form of latticed screens and wall panels, a form which had been evident in his architectural and decorative work from the beginning, although never so obsessive.

The demise of the long curves and the implicit animal-vegetable symbolism concurs more or less with the rapid disappearance of Art Nouveau ornament throughout Europe, but it is not likely that Mackintosh's abandonment of these forms can be attributed simply to a superficial change in taste. His own stated intentions were too serious to be diverted by such a change.

The growing dependence on straight lines did not indicate a waning interest in ornament itself. Indeed, these two interiors have less simple serenity than almost any of his earlier work.

During the time that these works were being carried out, Mackintosh's personal affairs were rapidly degenerating. The working routine at the office was becoming less and less bearable, and he was succeeding in antagonizing clients and colleagues alike. Keppie, who had become before this president of the Glasgow Institute of Architects, and was a leading professional figure in the city, had nothing in common architecturally with his wilful, brilliant partner, and had shown, all in all, a remarkable tolerance in their relationship. But now both partners clearly required an escape from one another. The end came in 1913 when Mackintosh resigned, ostensibly in protest over an office submission to a local competition.

It has been said that by this time Mackintosh was already displaying his search for release in alcohol, and that his supervision of the work at Auchenibert was less than wholly responsible. In the end, the completion of the work was entrusted to another architect.

At this point, the historian must tread very carefully. For it is around just such an issue that myths develop. There is no doubt that Mackintosh enjoyed his whisky; but then so did his partner John Keppie, who lived a very long and productive life; and so did much of the community, from theologians to architects. The notion of alcoholism is a very neat way of explaining away a watershed in a career. But to suggest that Mackintosh 'took to the bottle' and thus demolished his own future is not only glib, but manifestly untrue. The reminiscences of those who knew him later, and the powerful evidence of his work in later years, are more than enough to refute such an idea.

But the fact that he was under increasing stress, and that he was not able to cope with it, are equally true. There were clear reasons for strain. Perhaps the first, and the one which is most open to speculation, was his own personality. The picture of the man that emerges from the all too little evidence is of a tense and hypersensitive person – certainly of a man of forcible opinions and high idealism, capable of

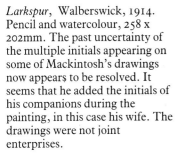

Larkspur, Walberswick, 1914. Pencil and watercolour, 258 x 202mm. The past uncertainty of the multiple initials appearing on some of Mackintosh's drawings now appears to be resolved. It seems that he added the initials of his companions during the painting, in this case his wife. The drawings were not joint enterprises.

Japonica, Chiddingstone, 1910.
Pencil and watercolour, 258 x
200mm.

immense expenditure of energy and of intense depression, warm-hearted and yet sensitive to criticism. He could respond with enthusiasm to support and to approbation, and perhaps even to outright personal opposition, but he was more and more being hamstrung by the obduracy of local officialdom, and by the lack of understanding and support of his peers.

In addition, he was not bringing a significant amount of work into the practice, and the relatively clear division of labour between the partners' jobs suggests a shared responsibility for generating new work.

The year following his resignation the Mackintoshes closed their Glasgow home and moved to the village of Walberswick on the Suffolk coast, where there was a small artists' colony frequented by the Newberys. While there, resting, painting and debating the uncertain future, war was declared and one possibility for Mackintosh's future was firmly eliminated. He had been invited to join his Continental friends, and was in correspondence with the Austrian Secessionists. Whether he ever seriously contemplated a permanent move of this kind is impossible to say, but the war in any event precluded it.

During this period in Walberswick Mackintosh concentrated considerable attention on a series of flower studies, undoubtedly the finest of his career. They were supposedly in preparation for a book to be published in Germany, a project which was forestalled by the outbreak of war. The quality of these works gives no indication of a man whose graphic skills had waned.

In 1915 the Mackintoshes moved to London and settled in rooms in Chelsea. But war had brought building to a standstill and they were without influential connections. Prospects were far from heartening. However, one potentially influential client did make contact with Mackintosh, although the circumstances of their meeting are not known. W. J. Bassett-Lowke was the proprietor of the well-known engineering and model-making firm of that name, and commissioned from Mackintosh a number of pieces of furniture, alterations to two houses, some small graphic works, and introduced Mackintosh to other friends. Of these, the most important project was the alteration, redecoration and furnishing of a small terraced house in Northampton, No. 78 Derngate, for Bassett-Lowke's own occupancy.

The interiors of the completed house are a startling departure from the Glasgow work, although they can be seen to link with the Cloister Room and the Chinese Tea Room in certain details. All hints of modelling and of the tense linear quality of his early work has disappeared, and been replaced by staccatto, hard-edged patterns which almost uncannily forecast decorative preoccupations of the next two decades. Here for the first time can be seen a direct indebtedness to Austrian work – Howarth has pointed out the source of the triangular patterning in the work of Josef Urban of Vienna, illustrated in *The Studio* special number on 'The Art Revival in Austria' published in 1906. But the indebtedness is not entirely Continental, for in the furniture particularly can be seen a clear

No. 78 Derngate, Northampton, 1916. The Hall.

relationship with such work as the later Gimson designs, and particularly Ambrose Heal's London furniture.

The narrow elevation to the garden was completely altered by Mackintosh, as a result of the provision of a small extension. Here the indebtedness to the Viennese is complete, and it could quite easily have been a product of Josef Hoffman or Adolf Loos. There is none of the particular Scottish character of Mackintosh's earlier work – which is hardly surprising in a terraced house in Northampton, nor is there any dependence on vernacular detailing. It is, of course, far too small a thing on which to base any judgement, but it does seem to represent the effort of the man to shake off the last vestiges of the past he had so irrevocably left behind him.

During the following years in Chelsea, the Mackintoshes occupied the bulk of their time with fabric designs, watercolours, and some small decorative commissions from Miss Cranston and other Glasgow friends including, in 1917, one more tea room interior, the Dug-Out, which connected with the Willow Tea Rooms but was actually built in an adjoining basement. They also engaged in various communal activities within the Chelsea artistic colony, including some theatrical design for 'The Plough', a short-lived but successful dramatic group. They were interesting but marginal activities, and they must have done little to restore Mackintosh's shaken equilibrium.

In 1920, however, a genuine architectural opportunity arrived. In rapid succession Mackintosh was requested by three artist friends in

Proposed artists' studios for the Arts League of Service, 1920. *Below* Elevation to Glebe Place, and *Right* elevation to Cheyne House Garden.

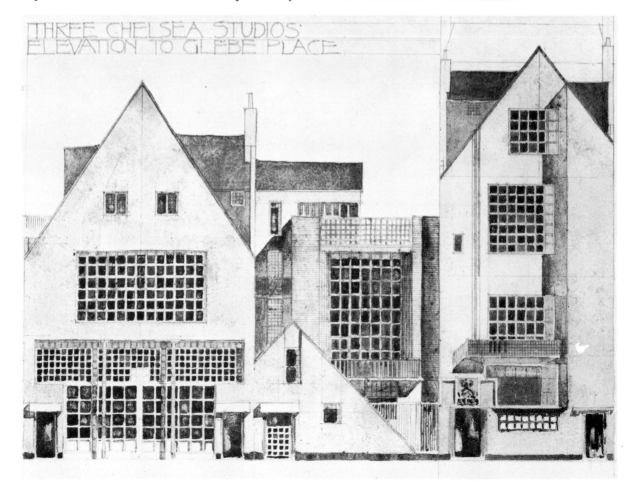

THREE CHELSEA STUDIOS
ELEVATION TO CHEYNE HOUSE GARDEN

the Chelsea community to design houses and studios, two of them on adjacent sites. Shortly thereafter Mackintosh was commissioned to design a block of studio flats for the Arts League of Service for a site adjoining two of the artists' premises, those of Derwent Wood and Harold Squire.

Although Squire and Wood were involved with the Arts League of Service, the three premises were on adjoining sites, and design work on all was proceeding concurrently, there is a curious absence of affinity between the various building elements in the group designs that emerged. The complexity of forms and the restlessness of the broken surfaces can be traced to the planning, and certainly to the rights-of-light requirements of adjoining properties. There is clearly the same driving determination to generate the building forms by the plan and its functional requirements, and in spite of the unfinished nature of the drawings and the absence of developed details, there is a latent and exciting power in the scheme. There are evidently traditional elements and materials, this time naturally enough the domestic traditions of old Chelsea rather than those of Scotland, mixed with Mackintosh's later decorative manner. There is also more than a passing affinity with C. R. Ashbee's Magpie and Stump houses in Cheyne Walk, with which Mackintosh was familiar.

But the scheme never came to fruition, although permission to build was eventually and reluctantly given by the Ecclesiastical Commissioners. The designs as they stand must be regarded, in the

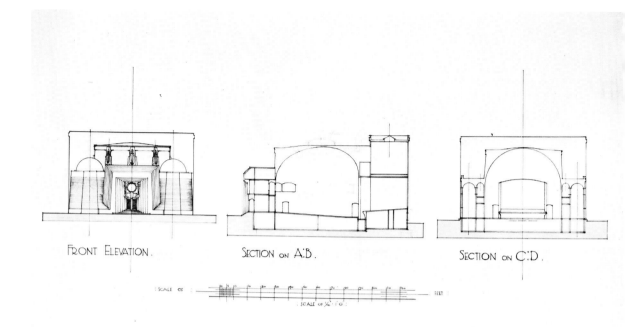

FRONT ELEVATION.

SECTION ON A·B·

SECTION ON C·D·

SCALE OF _____ FEET

SCALE OF ⅛ · 1· 0·

typical Mackintosh manner, as merely intentional, and what they might have become with his inventive and detailed shaping through the building process cannot be known. Whether, indeed, Mackintosh was any longer capable of the sustained driving effort required to carry out this process is questionable, although he did execute a smaller and quite different scheme for Harold Squire on the intended site. No precise description of the finished building is obtainable, but it does not appear to have been of major architectural interest, and Squire did not occupy it for long.

In the same year, 1920, Mackintosh was commissioned by Margaret Morris to design a theatre. His design was objected to strongly by the authorities, and without providing an alternative scheme, the project was eventually abandoned. The drawings indicate a formal, symmetrical disposition, with a relatively unadorned monumentality closely akin to the work of the Viennese Secessionists, not so much in detail as in feeling and intent. His current preoccupation with linear repetition and stepped surfaces can be seen in the immense and cavernous architrave around the main entrance, a form which can be related to, although only marginally justified by, the internal staircases. By and large, it is an assemblage of symmetrical forms which do not bear close functional inspection, a composition which relies far more on its image of 'modernity' and less on its generation by use than his mature Glasgow work.

Except for one or two small cottage designs during this period, Mackintosh's architectural work was finished. In the startling power of the Northampton interiors, the restless complexity of the Arts League of Service proposals, and the hard starkness of the theatre proposal, we are left with tantalizing glimpses of what might have been. The charm and prettiness had been bled from his work, but the latent power was more marked than ever. It is not surprising that he was not allowed to build again, but it is tragic. In the south, he was too old, too disenchanted, and too dispirited to begin a new rebellion. And the tide of taste and popular opinion was running too strongly in another direction to tolerate the 'foreign' experiments of a middle-

Design for a proposed theatre for Margaret Morris, 1920. Elevation and two sections. The firmly symmetrical, orthogonal treatment came very close to Vienna Secessionist feeling.

Right Le Fort Maillert, 1927. Watercolour, 358 x 285mm. The abstract build-up of flat planes and the carefully constructed composition owe little to traditional watercolour technique, but a great deal to Mackintosh's powerful architectural vision.

aged rebel. His only allies were those who, in the end, could not afford to build.

In 1923 the Mackintoshes left Chelsea and settled in Port Vendres on the Mediterranean coast of southern France. Here, for four years,

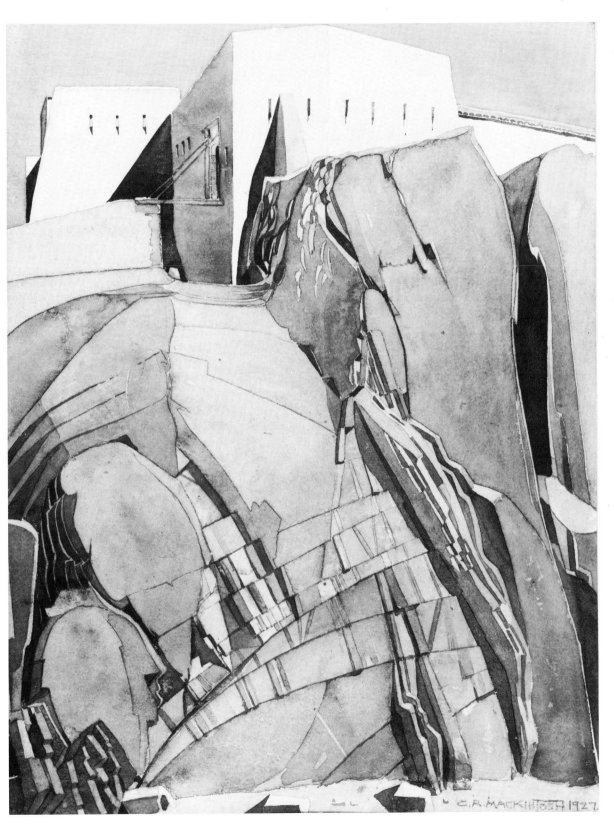

Charles devoted himself entirely to watercolour painting. The change of scene and the new pursuit had apparently been largely at Margaret's instigation; she had borne patiently and devotedly the years of trial and disappointment.

Right, top Wall decoration for No. 78 Derngate, Northampton.

The body of painting that was the product of these years at Port Vendres has been fully documented and described by Billcliffe. In the context of this narrative, they are of great interest. They are now the principal medium of his expressive purposes. They have, of course, a clear provenance in the architectural sketches he had been producing since his youth, and indeed, a painting of 1927 entitled *Le Fort Maillert* bears a remarkable resemblance to some of his sketches at Holy Island in 1902. But clearly his concern was no longer simply to record nature, or even some aspect of the natural scene, but to manipulate and shape the seen objects to his own purposes. And the inevitable irony of these paintings is that they are, above all things, architectural. Not only are they architectural in the deliberate and precise way that the elements are composed and built up, but the very forms and linear patterns betray a startling relationship with his later architectural designs. His 1927 study, *The Rocks*, for instance, can be directly compared with the detailing of the fireplace surround in the Bassett-Lowke interior, or indeed with the entrance architrave for Margaret Morris's theatre. And throughout these works is seen his life-long preoccupation with line and surface. Virtually devoid of modelling and of any atmospheric effects, whatever spatial effects they achieve are obtained through the implicit relationship of plane and line. The colours, too, are no longer the pale monochromatic arrangements with subtle accents, but rich, full and vital.

Seen in the context of his life's work, these paintings are the tangible evidence of an unrealized potential. They have all the graphic control and certainty that made the School of Art what it is. They have taken the idiom of his latest, and uncertain, architectural works and demonstrated that this manner, too, could be related directly to his touchstone, Nature. In a curious and poignant sense these paintings could have been built.

But this was no longer possible. In the autumn of 1927 Mackintosh complained of a sore throat and on medical advice returned with Margaret to London for specialist examination. Cancer of the tongue and throat was diagnosed, and he underwent radium treatment. He made a brief recovery and was released from hospital. But after some months he was admitted to a nursing home, where, on 10 December 1928, he died. Margaret Mackintosh did not survive her husband long. Four years later, on 10 January 1933, she died after a brief illness, in Chelsea.

In the University of Glasgow files, there is a small collection of letters relating to the disposition of the effects of the two studios after Margaret's death. Among the sad and concerned letters of a few friends is a terse and indifferent letter with an accompanying schedule from a firm of London valuers, listing the contents of the Chelsea studios. Furniture, personal effects, a large collection of sketches and architectural drawings, and thirty-one paintings were stated to be 'practically of no value', and the sum of £88 16s 2d was put on the total. Contributing to this total was a nominal value of £1 on four chairs of his own design. It would be unwise to moralize on the strength of market prices, but the letter and schedule seem an entirely consistent conclusion to the apathy of an era.

Right, bottom *La Rue du Soleil, Port Vendres*, 1927. Watercolour, 405 x 390mm. Even the water has been frozen into an architectural stillness, and not a sign of human life is to be seen.

144

CHAPTER NINE:
RETROSPECT

It is important to realize that the architectural work by which Mackintosh's reputation has been established was the product of little more than a single decade, begun by, and finishing with, the Glasgow School of Art. He sprang into being, almost fully formed, in 1896, and faded almost as quickly after 1906. His rise to prominence is entirely comprehensible in his ability, energy, and not more than the usual amount of good fortune. The reasons for his rapid decline are not nearly so simple.

Certainly his architectural isolation within his own generation must have been a major contributor to his disintegration. To understand this isolation, and in turn to understand the measure of his own contribution to the architectural picture of the times, some attempt must be made to delineate the major cross-currents of taste and ideals that prevailed during his working lifetime.

Underlying the theoretical developments outlined in the first chapter was a broad stream of rampant, undisciplined eclecticism, stimulated, particularly from 1870 onwards, by those serious theoreticians who were attempting to bring new relevance to their art by the principle of 'development' or 'absorption', but as practised by the ordinary and unconcerned practitioners, pastiches of the most extraordinary borrowings. It was an attitude of incredibly bemused optimism, captured precisely by A. E. Street, the not very distinguished son of the very distinguished Gothic Revivalist, G. E. Street, in an *Architectural Review* article of 1901 on 'Architecture in the Victorian Era':

The Purist of an earlier day would be shocked at the freedom and individuality with which the raw material of style is handled now, while the stickler for an ethical basis in architecture would hold his hands aloft to see the cheerful eclecticism with which the designer today skips from century to century, or stands with feet wide apart while the ages roll between. . . . If an elasticity of appreciativeness which will stretch to include examples of every style is to be aimed at, then we are near our mark.

This was hardly a state of affairs that would satisfy those seriously concerned with producing a coherent, recognizable architectural style for their time. And, from about 1894, a movement with just this intent was quickly gaining momentum. It was spearheaded by that ageing but still versatile master of image-making, Norman Shaw, and abetted by such younger devotees as Reginald Blomfield. With such designs as Chesters in Northumberland (1892), and Bryanston in Dorset (1890), Shaw heralded the return to the comparative order and respectability of the English Renaissance, and the younger men were quick to seize on its benefits. Here was the opportunity to

Port Vendres, La Ville, c 1924–26.
Watercolour, 460 x 460mm.

re-align architecture with academic taste and scholarship, to re-establish canons of proportion and of composition, and withal to pay lip service to the ideas of native tradition and indigenous development which had characterized the previous decades.

It was no coincidence that, concurrently with the rise of this neo-Renaissance movement, architectural education was finally becoming established in Britain as an academic discipline, and the profession itself was, through the medium of the Royal Institute of British Architects, slowly succeeding in defining for itself a legal, and a social, status. In the architecture of the English Renaissance could be found the basis for teaching, assessment and examination – in short, for regularized instruction in that most subjective of disciplines, design. Similarly, on the professional level, it provided an imagery which could be instantly recognized by society at large, and one which coincided with the notably self-conscious jingoism of the time.

This peculiar brand of national self-awareness was, at least in architecture, stimulated in part by the penetration of Britain's insularity. There was a growing awareness of the international prestige of the French Beaux Arts training, of the disciplined achievements of Germany, and even of the very substantial developments, technical and otherwise, of the upstart American cousins. In the case of the latter, there is almost an element of resentment that they were no longer dependent on the James Gibbs pattern books.

In all this, there was very little room for the William Morris social ideal of the band of happy craftsmen, all social distinctions gone, working together for the common weal. And there was little room either for the kind of abstract symbolism that had emerged out of the brief Art Nouveau exercises. And although Lethaby had, more than any other, fashioned a meaningful approach out of the Morris doctrine, it was foredoomed to failure under the weight of the prevailing ethos.

It was with those architects who, although not forming in any sense a cohesive school, linked most closely with the Morris and Lethaby ideology, that Mackintosh's early sympathy and admiration lay. His isolation from them, on the grounds of a quite misleading imagery, was an immeasurable loss to the architecture of the time.

Both Lethaby and Mackintosh, as has been seen, wrestled with the problem of an architectural iconography for the time. Mackintosh's solution was the natural outcome of his graphic interests, and, although he did not remain bound to the swirling lines and mystical symbolism of his early work, the attempt to 'decorate' in a way which related to both function and Nature can be seen to permeate his work unabated throughout his life.

Lethaby, on the other hand, although he abandoned the practice of architecture, had concluded relatively early, certainly before 1911, that the relevance of ornament had passed. He expressed this in the rewritten version of *Architecture, Mysticism and Myth* which was published serially in *The Builder* in 1928 as *Architecture, Nature and Magic*:

Ornamentation in its origins and growth was to protect and promote well-being. Now that the magic has gone out of it, unless some new content of nature and meaning is restored, it will die. Much is already dead, as we are slowly realising, and it will pass more and more out of the building customs of the future.

To a profession carefully building its public image and preening itself above all else on its artistic role in society, this was very cold fare indeed. And certainly Lethaby's proposal would have necessitated a professional revolution, and a revolution in training, as great as the social revolution required by Morris a generation earlier. No one, in any event, was interested in the idea of an architecture without 'style'. The functionalist stream, therefore, tended to revert to a kind of Arts and Crafts infancy, quite out of tune with the challenges and possibilities of the times, or to be absorbed into the neo-Renaissance revival that was developing. In its absorption into this stylistic construction, it lost the freedom and functional flexibility that had so excitingly begun to emerge in the latter part of the nineteenth century.

This, of course, was where Mackintosh's contribution was so relevant. For he developed an architectural idiom, which was firmly based on the British functional tradition, and yet which, by his graphic ability, was given a recognizable visual imagery. That this imagery, as it is seen in his early work, would be a fairly rapidly passing phase is evident by the way in which it had noticeably changed after 1904, and particularly in the very late works. But that does not destroy its importance. For what Mackintosh tangibly demonstrated was that a widely disparate set of threads, each of them in its way unique to the time, could be pulled together into a coherent architectural style, a style moreover that was capable of consistent and rapid development, and of all the functional flexibility, the capacity to absorb new functions and new materials, that had characterized the best of the earlier work.

The irony is that it was this very imagery, or at least its first manifestation, which was the cause of Mackintosh's isolation from his natural English brethren. And although the nature of this opposition has already been discussed, it must be stressed that the objection of the Lethaby group centred essentially on the very attempt to introduce a new 'style', and not the specific imagery of the style itself. They felt, and with some justification, that the pursuit of such a goal could only lead to the seduction away from the prior considerations of function and technique. What Mackintosh proved was that there was at least one man who could achieve all three.

It is entirely possible that the kind of synthesis that Mackintosh achieved could only have occurred in the relative separation of a provincial city, where an intimate knowledge of the rivalries and cross-currents that motivated various groups was perhaps not directly realized. But whether this is true or not, it is certain that, having developed this personal idiom, it had less practical chance of exploitation in a provincial city than in an ideological hotbed such as London, where his work could become directly known to those who shaped opinions. For it seems certain that had there been first-hand acquaintance with his work, there would have been immediate recognition of its motivation. One man who may, in fact, have recognized the intrinsic qualities of Mackintosh's work, and who certainly had at least some acquaintance with it, was Baillie Scott, who said in a lecture given on behalf of the Worshipful Company of Carpenters in 1908:

Do not be too ready to scorn what is called the 'New Art'. It is true the greater part of it is sorry stuff; but you will still find, amongst much that is affected and bizarre, here and there the right note struck: here and there the new thing which is also a good thing. It must also never be forgotten that all the old work we admire so much was new once, and when it first appeared it must have been as startling in its novelty as any of the products of the 'New Art' of our day.

This, from a dyed-in-the-wool Arts and Crafts man, was bordering on the heretical, and was certainly as enthusiastic a reception as could have been expected.

But, by and large, there was simply no interest in Mackintosh and his efforts. To the English architects, he was simply one of the Glasgow 'spook school', and, as one of the potpourri of novelties picked up by *The Studio*, not to be taken too seriously.

In spite of the early enthusiasm of many younger men, and the continued support of friends like the Newberys and Miss Cranston, there is no evidence to suggest that Mackintosh ever found any architectural 'soul mates' on the Glasgow scene. After the departure for Liverpool of Herbert MacNair, who never practised architecture in his own right, Mackintosh's closest friend professionally appears to have been James Salmon Jr., the son and grandson of established Glasgow architects. And although in Salmon's work many of the characteristic forms of the Glasgow Art Nouveau decorative details can be seen, they never effectively moved beyond the kind of work Mackintosh produced for Queen Margaret's Medical College.

Mackintosh's isolation in relation to the Continent was similar. Certainly he was not known to them on any scale until after the turn of the century, and, as has been noted, his exposure to the Europeans was almost entirely by means of exhibitions and limited decorative ventures.

Thus the remarkable fact is that while his mature style drew from many sources, he never had the benefit of an architectural 'dialogue' with like minds. Nor was he able to share with those who might have benefited his own developing ideas.

For it is entirely clear from his own work that his ideas did expand and develop rapidly during his most productive decade. At the outset he was much preoccupied with decorative symbolism, and it was this that led him so compulsively to the title and contents of Lethaby's book. But with the inception of the School of Art project, this symbolic interest became closely interwoven, with, and sometimes obscured by, the decorative possibilities of function and building structure. The graphically symbolic predilection continued, of course, and was particularly emphasized in the tea room projects, but even in these, the growing interest in the actual manipulation of the bones and sinews of the building structure can be seen. He was directly aware of these two constituent aspects himself. In his 1902 paper 'Seemliness' quoted in Chapter Six, he said:

The power which the artist possesses of representing objects to himself explains the hallucinating character of his work . . . their tendency towards symbolism – but the creative imagination is far more important. The artist cannot attain to mastery in his art unless he is endowed in the highest degree with the faculty of invention.

And this inventive capacity had to be centred on an '. . . understanding of the absolute and true requirements of a building or object'.

This inventive faculty, as manifested in the first wing of the School of Art, was characterized by the shaping of forms, the subtle modelling of timber, masonry and metal, that betrays craft-oriented, rather than technology-oriented thinking. This had nothing to do with relative plainness or embellishment, but with the actual forms of the pieces with which the assemblage was composed. Over the following decade, Mackintosh moved consciously towards a decorative inventiveness which relied much more on the cumulative effect of the assembly of pieces than on the forms of the pieces themselves. A comparison between the woodwork of the School of Art museum and the library interior makes this clear.

The few works that Mackintosh executed after leaving Glasgow show an unmistakable decline in his capacity, not surprisingly. But they do demonstrate the. continued decorative tendency in this direction, and in the final brief flowering of his talent in the water-colour paintings, a hint is shown of what it might have become in architectural terms.

One aspect of his times, however, with which Mackintosh never did come to terms, was the changed role of the architect in society. Although the profession had been established in more or less its present state by the time Mackintosh began, only during the last decades of the nineteenth century was it beginning to face the really demanding tasks of building for a growing variety of functions within strict limits of economy and performance. Problems of accounting (and accountability), of contract law, of specification and information were all constricting the artistic autonomy that the architect tended to feel – particularly if he read Ruskin – was his due. Within this more and more impersonal working framework, where every party to the building enterprise was constrained by documentation, it became a continuous battle for Mackintosh – and others of the same persuasion – to manipulate, refine and improve their projects as they developed. And the multiple frictions resulting from his insistence on doing just this must not be underestimated; they may well have been one of the major factors in his collapse.

What, then, was Mackintosh's influence on the architecture of his time? Effectively, none. His greatest admirers and constant supporters were the Austrian Secessionists. But while, as Howarth has pointed out, there are marginal evidences of his early decorative influence in some of their interior and furniture designs, his architectural roots were far removed from theirs. And in their eulogies of his design the emphasis is entirely on those decorative qualities which the historians of the modern movement in architecture have deplored. He had certainly none of the fundamental impact on European architecture that Frank Lloyd Wright, his contemporary, had through the Wasmuth publications of 1910.

In Britain, his architectural eclipse was total. He can scarcely, therefore, be considered a pioneer of modern architecture in the usual sense of having contributed to a developing collective ideology, or even to a developing vocabulary of form.

But he was not, therefore, a total phenomenon, an isolated genius without ancestry or progeny. He was rather a last and remote efflorescence of a vital British tradition which reached back to Pugin. He could not perhaps have existed apart from his isolation, but he could not in the end have any succession because of it. With his pursuit of the 'modern', his love of the old, and his obsessive individuality, he was one of the last and one of the greatest of the Victorians.

ACKNOWLEDGMENTS

The accumulation of knowledge in and around Glasgow about the life and work of Charles Rennie Mackintosh is formidable. But the enthusiasm and openness displayed to enquirers is equally remarkable. I have incurred many debts of gratitude to a number of people during the preparation of this book, as indeed I did more than fifteen years ago. As with that previous project, the late Sir Harry and Lady Barnes provided me with hospitality, help and genuine encouragement. Everyone connected with the Charles Rennie Mackintosh Society owes much to Patricia Douglas, the Society Secretary, and she has been more than generous to my editors and myself with time and information. I am grateful to Roger Billcliffe for his generous sharing of his own research and judgements. Professor Andrew Macmillan has been typically hospitable, critical and perceptive and has welcomed my intrusions. The staff at the Hunterian Art Gallery, in particular Pamela Reekie, have gone out of their way to provide material for my editors and myself. It was very reassuring to have Keith Gibson helping again with the black and white photographs and I was most grateful to Douglas Corrance for his care and perceptive eye in providing the colour. Bettina Tayleur has shepherded the project through its various phases with thoroughness and enthusiasm, which never clouded her meticulous judgement, and with remarkably good-natured tolerance of the shortcomings of her author. There are many others who have provided help in a variety of ways, and to all of them I offer thanks, even though I cannot name them all. There is one, however, who, during a somewhat overburdened and difficult period, supported, picked up behind me and made the time and space for this work. To my wife, Marilyn, I owe much more than a dedication can begin to signify.

PICTURE CREDITS

BIBLIOGRAPHY

For both the serious scholar and the more general reader access to the extant information on Mackintosh is now relatively easy. The available information falls into two categories: principal buildings, furnishings, interiors and paintings; and the published documentary sources. I have therefore divided the list of sources into two groups.

1. PLACES

Charles Rennie Mackintosh Society Queen's Cross, 870 Garscube Road, Glasgow G20. Telephone: 041-946 6600
Hon. Secretary: Patricia Douglas
The Society is housed in the former Queen's Cross Church designed by Mackintosh, and not only provides a starting point for access to Mackintosh buildings and collections, but also offers relevant publications, memorabilia and help to enquirers. The Newsletter is described below.

Hunterian Art Gallery The University, Glasgow G12 8QQ. Telephone: 041-339 8855
Curator: Pamela Reekie
The new Gallery contains a substantial reconstruction of the principal interiors of the Charles and Margaret Mackintosh home at 78 Southpark Avenue, as well as original documents, drawings and pictorial records. The display also features a re-creation of the guest bedroom at 78 Derngate, Northampton.

Glasgow School of Art 167 Renfrew Street, Glasgow G3 6RQ. Telephone: 041-332 9797
Director: Professor Anthony Jones
This is the principal monument to the Mackintosh architectural genius. The building contains an astonishing amount of the original fittings, furnishings and decorative works, as well as important documents.

Museum and Art Galleries Argyle Street, Kelvingrove, Glasgow G3 8AG. Telephone: 041-334 1134
The Art Gallery contains a major collection of Mackintosh's work.

For access to further Mackintosh buildings and works, both those in public and private hands, the reader is referred to the Charles Rennie Mackintosh Society listed above, where up-to-date information is always available.

2. PUBLICATIONS

As in recent publications on Mackintosh, the reader is referred to the comprehensive catalogue produced by Thomas Howarth in the second edition of *Charles Rennie Mackintosh and the Modern Movement*, Routledge & Kegan Paul, London, 1977. However a number of important studies have been published since then, as indicated below.

Billcliffe, Roger
 Architectural Sketches and Flower Drawings by Charles Rennie Mackintosh. Academy Editions, London, 1977.
 Mackintosh Watercolours. John Murray, London, 1978/Taplinger, New York, 1978.
 Charles Rennie Mackintosh: The Complete Furniture, Furniture Drawings and Interior Designs. Lutterworth Press, London, 1979; second edition 1980.
 Mackintosh Textile Designs. John Murray, London, 1982.
In these definitive catalogues, Billcliffe has provided an immensely impressive and careful description of the Mackintosh *oeuvre*. They are a delight to the eye as well as a tribute to thorough scholarship.

Charles Rennie Mackintosh Society:
 Newsletters 1973–present. These Newsletters have published papers of substance, both on issues relating directly to Mackintosh and on his contemporary context. Where reference is made in the text to a particular paper or author, the Newsletter number is given.

Kimura, Hiroaki
 Charles Rennie Mackintosh: Architectural Drawings Catalogue and Design Analytical Catalogue. Unpublished.
Although unpublished, this thesis is a major contribution to Mackintosh studies, and has filled many gaps, in particular concerning his architectural contribution to Honeyman & Keppie.

CHRONOLOGY

The Chronology indicates the principal events in the life of Charles Rennie Mackintosh. Dates for such events as his birth and marriage can be precise; for such activities as design and building they are necessarily more uncertain, since the intervals between first design, detail design, construction (and often further design and redesign) can span several years and are not often clearly recorded or differentiated. The most comprehensive record of Mackintosh's architectural activities is contained in the unpublished thesis of Hiroaki Kimura, listed under *Bibliography*. The most complete record of his activities in furniture design, painting and fabrics can be found in the Billcliffe publications.

1868

Born, June 7, Glasgow.

1884

Began professional training with John Hutchison, Glasgow.

Commenced classes at Glasgow School of Art.

1887

Awarded two prizes by Glasgow Institute of Architects.

1889

Joined Honeyman and Keppie, Glasgow, where he met Herbert MacNair (1868–1955).

Awarded one of Queen's Prizes, South Kensington, for design of a Presbyterian Church.

1890

Awarded Alexander Thomson Scholarship for design of a public hall.

Awarded National Silver Medal, South Kensington, for design of a museum of science and art.

1891

Trip to Italy: Naples, Palermo, Rome, Orvieto, Siena, Florence, Pisa, Pistoia, Bologna, Ravenna, Venice, Padua, Vicenza, Verona, Mantua, Cremona, Brescia, Bergamo, Lake Como, Milan, Pavia. Return via Paris and Antwerp.

Paper on *Scottish Baronial Architecture* read to the Glasgow Architectural Association.

1892

Designs for a chapter house for Soane Medallion Competition; awarded National Gold Medal, South Kensington, for this design.

Paper, *Italy*, read to Glasgow Architectural Association.

1892–93

The Glasgow Art Club (interiors and extension). Project by Honeyman & Keppie. Keppie partner in charge; details left to Mackintosh.

Canal Bargemen's Institute.

1893

Glasgow Herald Building designed.

Project for a railway terminus for Soane Medallion Competition.

Paper, *Architecture*, read to Glasgow Institute of Architects.

1893–94

Alterations to the entrance hall and library at Craigie Hall, Glasgow.
    Commissioned by Thomas Mason. Project by Keppie; Mackintosh responsible for designing fittings.

1894–96

Queen Margaret's Medical College, Glasgow.

1895

Martyrs Public School, Glasgow.

Interiors at Gladsmuir, Kilmacolm.

Lennox Castle Inn, Lennoxtown.

1896

Glasgow School of Art Competition.

1896–97

The Buchanan Street Tea Rooms, Glasgow (stencil decorations).
    Commissioned by Miss Catherine Cranston; decoration work carried out by the firm of George Walton.

1897–99

Queen's Cross Church, Glasgow.

1897

The Argyle Street Tea Rooms, Glasgow (furniture).
    Commissioned by Miss C. Cranston.

Music Room at Craigie Hall, Glasgow (organ and fireplace).
    Commissioned by Thomas Mason.

Building begins at Glasgow School of Art.

1898

Project for Glasgow International Exhibition, 1901.

Ruchill St. Church Halls, Glasgow.

Dining-room for H. Bruckmann, Munich.

Bedroom at Westdel, Queen's Palace, Glasgow.
    Commissioned by J. Maclehose.

1898–99

Extension to office premises at 233 Vincent Street, Glasgow.

1899

Queen's Cross Church, Glasgow (furniture designed and church opened for worship).

Glasgow School of Art (east wing completed).

Frances Macdonald and Herbert MacNair married.

1899–1900

Ruchill Street Free Church Hall.

1900

120 Mains Street, Glasgow (interiors and furniture at own flat).

Dunglass Castle, Bowling (interiors and furniture).
    Commissioned by Macdonald family.

The White Dining Room, Ingram Street Tea Rooms, Glasgow (interiors and furniture).
    Commissioned by Miss C. Cranston.

Room for the Eighth Exhibition of the Vienna Secession.

Windyhill, Kilmacolm.
    Commissioned by William Davidson Jr.

Married Margaret Macdonald.

1901

The *Haus eines Kunstfreundes* Competition.
    Drawings awarded purchase prize of 600 marks.

Windyhill, Kilmacolm, completed (and furniture).

Daily Record Office, Glasgow.

Stands designed for Glasgow International Exhibition.

Gate Lodge, Auchenbothie, Kilmacolm.

Further rooms at Ingram Street Tearooms.

1901–02

14 (now 34) Kingsborough Gardens, Glasgow (interiors and furniture).
    Commissioned by Mrs Rowat.

1902

The International Exhibition of Modern Decorative Art, Turin (design of stalls and room settings for Scottish section).

Liverpool Cathedral competition drawings.

The Wärndorfer Music Salon, Vienna.
    Commissioned by Fritz Wärndorfer.

1902–03

Exhibition Room, Moscow.

1903

The Willow Tea Rooms, Glasgow (exteriors and interiors).
    Commissioned by Miss C. Cranston.

1903–04

The Hill House, Helensburgh.
    Commissioned by Walter W. Blackie.

Interiors and furniture for Hous'hill, Nitshill, commenced.

1903–05

Shop and house above, Comrie, Perthshire.
    Commissioned by P. McPherson.

1904

Hous'hill, Nitshill, Glasgow (interiors and furniture).
    Commissioned by Miss C. Cranston and Major Cochrane.

Willow Tea Rooms opened.

Mackintosh becomes partner in the firm, now styled Honeyman, Keppie & Mackintosh.

Scotland Street School, Glasgow.

Chancel furniture for Holy Trinity Church, Bridge of Allan.

1904–05

Additions at Arddaroch near Loch Goil, Dumbartonshire.
  Commissioned by Brooman White.

Shop at 233 Sauchiehall Street for Messrs Henry and Carruthers.

1905

Dining-room for A. S. Ball exhibit, Berlin.

Furniture designed for Hous'hill and Windyhill.

Fireplace designed for Miss Rowat, Paisley.

1906

The Board Room, Glasgow School of Art.
  Commissioned by the School Governors.

Moved to 78 Southpark Avenue, Glasgow (designed exterior alterations and interiors).

1906–07

Commenced design for Mosside, Kilmacolm (first stage).

The Dutch Kitchen, Argyle Street Tea Rooms, Glasgow (conversion).
  Commissioned by Miss C. Cranston.

1906–08

Auchenibert, Killearn.
  Commissioned by F. J. Shand.

1907

The Oak Room, Ingram Street Tea Rooms (interiors and furniture).
  Commissioned by Miss C. Cranston.

The Moss, Dumgoyne (extension and fittings).

Building of west wing of Glasgow School of Art commenced.

1908

Alterations to the Lady Artists' Club, 5 Blythswood Square, Glasgow.

1908–10

Mosside, Kilmacolm (second stage).

1909

The Card Room at Hous'hill, Nitshill, Glasgow (furniture and fittings).
  Commissioned by Miss C. Cranston and Major Cochrane.

Interiors in the western half of Glasgow School of Art completed.

1909–10

The Oval Room and Ladies' Rest Room, Ingram Street Tea Rooms, Glasgow.
  Commissioned by Miss C. Cranston.

1911

The White Cockade Tea Room at the Glasgow Exhibition.

The Chinese Room and The Cloister Room, Ingram Street Tea Rooms, Glasgow.
  Commissioned by Miss C. Cranston.

1913

Alterations at Mosside, Kilmacolm.

Left Honeyman and Keppie.

1914

Visit to Walberswick.

Left Glasgow and moved to Walberswick.

1915

Moved to Chelsea.

1916

78 Derngate, Northampton (conversion of terraced house).
  Commissioned by Mr W. J. Bassett-Lowke.

Fabric designs for Messrs Foxton and Messrs Sefton, London.

1917

Bedroom for Sidney Horstmann, Bath.

The Dug-Out, Willow Tea Rooms, Sauchiehall Street, Glasgow (designed basement tea room).
  Commissioned by Miss C. Cranston.

Furniture for W. J. Bassett-Lowke, Mr W. Franklin and Mr F. Jones.

1918–19

Furniture and decoration at Candida Cottage, Roade, near Northampton, for W. J. Bassett-Lowke; for F. Jones at The Drive, Northampton, and for W. Franklin.

1919

The guest bedroom, 78 Derngate, Northampton (furniture and decorations).
　　Commissioned by W. J. Bassett-Lowke.

Cottage at East Grinstead for E. O. Hoppé, alterations and extensions.

Memorial fireplace for The Dug-Out, Willow Tea Rooms.

1920

New stencil decorations in the hall, 78 Derngate, Northampton.
　　Commissioned by W. J. Bassett-Lowke.

Design for studios, studio flats for the Arts League of Service and a theatre for Margaret Morris.

1921

Book covers for Blackie & Sons.

1923

Trip to Port Vendres

Settled in South of France.

1924

Visit to Amélie-les-Bains.

1925

Visit to Mont Louis.

1927

Returned to London.

1928

Died of cancer of the tongue.

1933

Margaret Macdonald died.

Memorial Exhibition organized in Glasgow.

INDEX